Go weeping

Ps. 126:6 sheaves

Precious Seed

OUTREACH FOR

THE UNREACHED

A. V. WASHBURN

Convention Press

NASHVILLE, TENNESSEE

Code Number: Church Study Course for Teaching and Training
This book is number 1726 in category 17, section A.

Library of Congress Catalog Card Number: 60-12434
Printed in the United States of America
105. AL 60 R.R.D.

TO DR. J. N. BARNETTE
Whose Unselfish Service, Deep Insights into the
Ministry of the Sunday School, Personal Friendship and
Encouragement Have Been a Blessing to Me
and

TO MY FELLOW WORKERS
In the Sunday School Department and in the State
Departments with Whom It Is a Rare Privilege to Serve
This Book Is Gratefully Dedicated

About the Author

A. V. WASHBURN was born in Cleveland County, North Carolina. He graduated from Boiling Springs High School, Boiling Springs, North Carolina (1929), and from Wake Forest College, Wake Forest, North Carolina, where he received the B.A. degree (*magna cum laude*) in 1933. He holds the M.A. degree from Peabody College, Nashville, Tennessee. He also studied at Southern Baptist Theological Seminary, Louisville, Kentucky, and did graduate work at Southwestern Baptist Theological Seminary, Fort Worth, Texas. He holds an honorary Doctor of Letters (Litt.D.) degree from Georgetown College, Georgetown, Kentucky.

On January 1, 1958, Dr. Washburn became secretary of the Sunday School Department of the Baptist Sunday School Board and editor of *The Sunday School Builder*.

Dr. Washburn's work experience includes service as class officer, teacher, department superintendent, and general superintendent. He did summer field work in North Carolina from 1929–32. He served in the Sunday School Department of the Baptist Sunday School Board as associate in charge of Young People's work 1933–43 and as secretary of teaching and training 1946–58, when he was elected secretary of the Sunday School Department.

He is a member of the Baptist Jubilee Advance Committee of the Southern Baptist Convention, the Curriculum Committee of the Inter-Agency Council, the Church Study Course Committee, and the Curriculum Committee of the Baptist Sunday School Board. He is author of the book *Young People in the Sunday School*.

Mrs. Washburn was the former Ethel Kate Allison of Sylva, North Carolina. They have three children, Ann (now Mrs. Terry Davis), Kent, and Janet.

CONTENTS

Church Study Course for Teaching and Training

THE CHURCH STUDY COURSE FOR TEACHING AND TRAINING began October 1, 1959. It is a merger of three courses previously promoted by the Sunday School Board—the Sunday School Training Course, the Graded Training Union Study Course, and the Church Music Training Course.

The course is fully graded. The system of awards provides a series of five diplomas of twenty books each for Adults or Young People, one diploma of ten books for Young People, two diplomas of five books each for Intermediates, and two diplomas of five books each for Juniors. Book awards earned previously in the Sunday School Training Course, the Graded Training Union Study Course, and the Church Music Training Course may be transferred to the new course.

The course is comprehensive, with books grouped into nineteen categories. The purpose of the course is to (1) help Christians to grow in knowledge and conviction; (2) help them to grow toward maturity in Christian character and competence for service; (3) encourage them to participate worthily as workers in their churches; and (4) develop leaders for all phases of church life and work.

The Church Study Course for Teaching and Training is promoted by the Baptist Sunday School Board, 127 Ninth Avenue, North, Nashville, Tennessee, through its Sunday School, Training Union, Church Music, and Church Administration departments, and by these same departments in the states affiliated with the Southern Baptist Convention. A complete description of the course and the system of awards may be found in the *Church Study Course for Teaching and Training* catalog, which may be obtained without charge from any one of these departments.

A record of all awards earned should be maintained in each church. A person should be designated by the church to keep the files. Forms for such records may be ordered from any Baptist Book Store.

Requirements for Credit in Class or Home Study

IF CREDIT IS DESIRED for the study of this book in a class or by home study, the following requirements must be met:

I. IN CLASSWORK

1. The class must meet a minimum of seven and one-half clock hours. The required time does not include assembly periods. Ten class periods of forty-five minutes each are recommended. (If laboratory or clinical work is desired in specialized or technical courses, this requirement may be met by six clock hours of class-work and three clock hours of supervised laboratory or clinical work.)

2. A class member who attends all class sessions and completes the reading of the book within a week following the last class session will not be required to do any written work.

3. A class member who is absent from one or more class sessions must answer the questions (pp. 150–151) on all chapters he misses. In such a case, he must turn in his paper within a week, and he must certify that he has read the book.

4. The teacher should request an award for himself. A person who teaches a book in section B, C, or D of any category or conducts an approved unit of instruction for Nursery, Beginner, or Primary children will be granted an award in category 11, Special Studies, which will count as an elective on his own diploma. He should specify in his request the name of the book taught, or the unit conducted for Nursery, Beginner, or Primary children.

5. The teacher should complete the "Request for Book Awards —Class Study" (Form 150) and forward it within two weeks after the completion of the class to the Church Study Course Awards Office, 127 Ninth Avenue, North, Nashville 3, Tennessee.

II. IN HOME STUDY

1. A person who does not attend any class session may receive credit by answering all questions for written work as indicated in

the book (pp. 150–151). When a person turns in his paper on home study, he must certify that he has read the book.

2. Students may find profit in studying the text together, but individual papers are required. Carbon copies or duplicates in any form cannot be accepted.

3. Home study work papers may be graded by the pastor or a person designated by him, or they may be sent to the Church Study Course Awards Office for grading. The form entitled "Request for Book Awards—Home Study" (Form 151) must be used in requesting awards. It should be mailed to Church Study Course Awards Office, 127 Ninth Avenue, North, Nashville 3, Tennessee.

III. CREDIT FOR THIS BOOK

This book is number 1726 in category 17, section A.

CHAPTER 1

I. IN THE MIDST OF MULTITUDES

    1. God's Heart Is with the Multitudes

    2. Christ's Compassion Is for the Multitudes

    3. The Church's Mission Is to the Multitudes

II. OUTREACH FOR THE UNREACHED

    1. Outreach Is in the Purpose of God's Grace

    2. Outreach Was in the Preaching of the Prophets

    3. Outreach Is in the Compassion of Jesus

    4. Outreach Is the Command of Christ

    5. Outreach Must Be in the Mission of Our Churches

III. THE MULTIPLYING MULTITUDES AROUND US

    1. Population Increases

    2. Urgency Grows

    3. Population Makes Demands

IV. A CHURCH'S CONTACT WITH THE MULTITUDES

    1. A Church Has the Message and Mission

    2. The Message Must Reach the People

V. WHAT SHALL WE DO FOR THE MULTITUDES?

1

Churches in the Midst of the Multitudes

AMERICA is a land of churches! Great new churches, beautiful and adequate, proclaim the vision, faith, and dedication of those who planned and built them. Old churches with weather-marked walls speak of long years of witness to a hard and needy world. Small "first unit" churches dot the landscape of the expanding population centers and affirm the vitality of the Christian faith to claim new communities for Christ! The modest little church on the hill or by the brook in the peaceful countryside speaks of the refreshing, sustaining love of God for his people everywhere!

The major task of individual Christians and churches has not changed since New Testament days. As members who make up the Southern Baptist churches, we are placed "in the midst of a crooked and perverse nation" in order to "shine as lights in the world; holding forth the word of life" (Phil. 2:15–16).

I. IN THE MIDST OF MULTITUDES

Nothing short of an all-out conquest for people is adequate for churches today. For this conquest Christ has planted his churches in the midst of unreached multitudes.

1. God's Heart Is with the Multitudes

Until God's motive is our motive, his concern our concern, we will do little about the opportunities around us. Consider these motivating words:

1

"For God so loved the world, that he gave his only begotten Son, that whosoever believeth in him should not perish, but have everlasting life" (John 3:16).

"Gather the people together, men, and women, and children, and thy stranger that is within thy gates, that they may hear, and that they may learn, and fear the Lord your God, and observe to do all the words of this law: and that their children, which have not known any thing, may hear, and learn to fear the Lord your God, as long as ye live in the land whither ye go over Jordan to possess it" (Deut. 31:12-13).

"As my Father hath sent me, even so send I you" (John 20:21).

"For the Son of man is come to seek and to save that which was lost" (Luke 19:10).

"Come ye after me, and I will make you to become fishers of men" (Mark 1:17).

"Say not ye, There are yet four months, and then cometh harvest? behold, I say unto you, Lift up your eyes, and look on the fields; for they are white already to harvest" (John 4:35).

2. *Christ's Compassion Is for the Multitudes*

Jesus, being in the midst of the multitudes was, and is, the compassionate Saviour. It is interesting and revealing to consider how various individuals react to the multitudes. Sometimes great crowds of people bring excitement. At other times, as when one is in a strange city, they simply disturb the soul and accentuate loneliness.

For Jesus, the needy multitudes constituted his task. They were the ripe harvest which he had come to garner for the Father. They were not the dismay of the Saviour. They were the reason for his coming into the world.

Some leaders of the day saw sinful men as a diseased portion of humanity that should not be touched—unclean and unwanted. Such was the attitude of the Pharisees, but not of Jesus. Some thought of the multitudes as existing to serve the purposes of the rulers. Such may have been the feeling of the high priests, but not of Jesus. Some considered the multitudes as just so much capital to be exploited. Such was the practice of the money-changers in the Temple, but not of Jesus. The multitudes moved his heart to compassion. "The Son of man is come to seek and to save that which was lost" (Luke 19:10).

In a few crisp words, Jesus conveyed to his disciples something of his concern as he saw the multitudes of men and women everywhere he went. In all the cities and villages, in the synagogues where he taught, in every street or hovel where he healed the bodies of the diseased, Jesus could not escape the needs of the scattered, distressed multitudes. "Therefore said he unto them, The harvest truly is great, but the labourers are few: pray ye therefore the Lord of the harvest, that he would send forth labourers into his harvest" (Luke 10:2).

3. *The Church's Mission Is to the Multitudes*

Years ago, an Episcopal clergyman was speaking to a group of Baptist friends. They were talking about the vast difference in the number of Baptists and Baptist churches in comparison with the Episcopal congregations. Finally, the Episcopalian said: "When our church fathers came into the area, the uppermost question in their minds was, Where are the churches? When the Baptist preachers came on the scene, their chief question was, Where are the people?"

Indeed, that is a difference—a tremendous difference—in viewpoint and in approach. Surely, it is one very practical reason why the number of Southern Baptist churches has grown to approximately thirty-two thousand and the number of Southern Baptists to more than nine million in a few brief generations.

(1) *Churches must be rightly located.*—If a church is to

reach the maximum number of people, then the physical location of the building becomes extremely important. It should be placed where it will be seen and used by the largest number of people. As Ernest B. Myers has said:

There is logic in placing the church on property easily accessible to the people. The church building should never be located on a side street or behind other buildings. We are in business to reach people. If we hide the church, we are hiding the lighthouse that has been built to help the helpless find their way to safety.

(2) *Churches must be spiritually attuned to the needs of people.*—In keeping with the spirit of Christ and the purpose of our churches, we must ever stay in the midst of the multitudes. Always Christ is concerned with people—the multitudes—and with the abounding life that is available to all who will receive it.

> Where cross the crowded ways of life,
>   Where sound the cries of race and clan,
> Above the noise of selfish strife,
>   We hear Thy voice, O Son of man!
>
> In haunts of wretchedness and need,
>   On shadow'd thresholds dark with fears,
> From paths where hide the lures of greed,
>   We catch the vision of Thy tears.
>
> O Master, from the mountain side,
>   Make haste to heal the hearts of pain;
> Among these restless throngs abide;
>   O tread the city's streets again.
>
> FRANK MASON NORTH

(3) *Church members must accept responsibility for people.*—Two great convictions must literally dominate every Christian today—the multiplying millions of lost people that abound everywhere and the matchless power in Christ to transform them.

Time is running out! So say the scientist and statesman;

so say preacher and politician. Surely, time is running out for nations—for peoples of the earth to learn to live together in peace. Time is certainly running out for many people yet unreached for Christ. Let us not fail them—or fail our opportunities to serve the cause of our Saviour. As we face this fateful hour, we must all understand more fully the urgency of our Christian conquest. We must know that it is not a responsibility that a few leaders alone can meet.

At such an hour as we now face, Moses stood before the people of Israel as their leader. They were on their way to claim the new land that God had promised them. The journey was rough and long. The obstacles were many and difficult. The discouragements were persistent, and success seemed far away. Moses was tired and disappointed.

But something happened! Look, if you will, at the account in the eleventh chapter of Numbers. Moses, the leader, is pouring out his heart to the Lord! "Wherefore . . . the burden of all this people upon me? . . . I am not able to bear all this people alone, because it is too heavy for me" (Num. 11:11–14).

But God had never intended that Moses should bear all of this responsibility alone. "And the Lord said unto Moses, Gather unto me seventy men of the elders of Israel, . . . and I will take of the spirit which is upon thee, and will put it upon them; and they shall bear the burden of the people with thee, that thou bear it not thyself alone" (Num. 11:16–17).

What do we learn from this experience of Moses? First of all, that God's work is seldom a one-man job. When seventy more people were enlisted, the Holy Spirit had seventy more channels through which to work.

The lesson is surely meant for leaders today. It is the old story of heart concern. Moses felt the burden of people lying heavily across his heart. It was something that he could not escape—and would not if he could. It was an assignment from God, and not a self-chosen task. But it was a task in which Moses was to enlist others.

Here we stand before a host of unreached people, to lead them through Bible study to find Christ as Saviour and Lord. Surely, we today feel acutely the responsibility of such a task and accept it as a burden of our souls. Do we feel just as keenly our responsibility for enlisting fellow Christians in our churches to share in the task?

II. OUTREACH FOR THE UNREACHED

Late one evening, I was listening to a religious program on the car radio. Suddenly a phrase caught and held my attention! "Share in our outreach for the unreached!"

That says it for all of us, does it not? That is what our work is all about! "Outreach for the Unreached" clarifies our objective and helps to focus our energies on the crucial need of our churches.

1. *Outreach Is in the Purpose of God's Grace*

"Outreach for the Unreached" involves the whole plan of the redeeming grace of God—reaching, teaching, winning, and developing. It gives an essential thrust to the wholesale obligation of the work entrusted to the churches. True, we must think in terms of individuals, because a single individual is the object of the love of God. In this sense the work of our churches is a retail operation. But what God has done for one soul, he has done for everyone who will accept the terms and meet the requirements. We must also be concerned with the wholesale aspects of our assignment. We must think of multitudes.

Early in the record, God's plan for the redemption of a lost world was made evident. We see it in the messianic prophecy: "And I will put enmity between thee and the woman, and between thy seed and her seed; it shall bruise thy head, and thou shalt bruise his heel" (Gen. 3:15). We hear it in the word to Abraham: "In thee shall all families of the earth be blessed" (Gen. 12:3). Jesus clarified this outreaching purpose of God in the words: "Even so it is not the will of your Father which is in heaven, that one of these little ones should perish" (Matt. 18:14).

God has not found it easy to get his people to keep outreach paramount in their plans. Jonah, for example, was commanded to preach to the sinful city of Nineveh. Yet it was only after a terrifying and unsuccessful experience of trying to run from his obligation that the prophet was willing to go in keeping with the purpose of God.

Could it be that God had no greater problem with Jonah in this respect than he has with many in our churches today? Could it be that the spirit of satisfaction with what we are now reaching is just as much a denial of the basic command of God as was the overt act of Jonah in trying to run the other way when God would send him to Nineveh!

2. *Outreach Was in the Preaching of the Prophets*

In the writings of the Old Testament prophets, we find evidence that God was embracing all men in his purpose of redemption. Isaiah, through his preaching, kept alive the responsibility of God's people to extend his blessings to others. "I will gather all nations and tongues; and they shall come, and see my glory. . . . And they shall bring all your brethren for an offering unto the Lord out of all nations" (Isa. 66:18–20).

The prophet's call for enlargement is particularly appropriate to every church today: "Enlarge the place of thy tent, and let them stretch forth the curtains of thine habitations: spare not, lengthen thy cords, and strengthen thy stakes" (Isa. 54:2).

Good Sermon Text.

3. Outreach Is in the Compassion of Jesus

Never is any lost soul beyond the compassionate concern of the Saviour. Jesus went throughout the cities and villages teaching and ministering to the physical needs of the people. "But when he saw the multitudes, he was moved with compassion on them, because they fainted, and were scattered abroad, as sheep having no shepherd" (Matt. 9:36). Jesus called on his disciples to get a vision of the lost multitudes: "Lift up your eyes, and look on the fields; for they are white already to harvest" (John 4:35).

4. Outreach Is the Command of Christ

The risen Lord spelled out clearly to his followers their responsibility for a continuing outreach. He had declared his purpose as seeking and saving the lost and giving them the privilege of abundant life. Now that Christ had completed his ministry on earth, his followers were to take the good news of redemption to lost men everywhere. They should and they must, under divine command! "Then said Jesus to them again, Peace be unto you: as my Father hath sent me, even so send I you" (John 20:21).

5. Outreach Must Be in the Mission of Our Churches

There is nothing small, ordinary, or limited in the mission assigned to our churches. Listen! "All power . . . Go ye . . . teach . . . baptizing . . . teaching them . . . all things"! These power-packed, action-filled, sharply defined words leave us no option. Churches, in every aspect of their work, must "move at his command"!

III. The Multiplying Multitudes Around Us

Something is happening in the world that is difficult to assess completely and accurately. It is our breath-taking population increase. A statement released in 1959 by the United Nations informs us that from the beginning of man's existence in the world until the present, the aggregate population has reached two and a half billion people. At the present rate of increase, it will require only thirty years to add another two billion to the world's population! The implications for government, for economics, for our churches are beyond calculation! "The growth of the world population during the next twenty-five years has an importance which transcends economic and social considerations. It is at the very heart of the problem of our existence."

If the heart of Jesus was moved within him as he was seeing the multitudes of two thousand years ago, how his heart must go out now to the multiplied millions today!

1. Population Increases

What is happening to the population in America? Quoting J. P. Edmunds, statistician at the Baptist Sunday School Board:

Our population in 1959 was approximately one hundred seventy-nine million people. By 1970 it is expected to be two hundred nine million; and by 1980, two hundred sixty million. This increase is like adding a new Chicago, Illinois, and a Flint, Michigan, to our population every year for twenty years. When you consider that there will likely be eighty-one million more people in 1980 than now, and the fact that our Sunday schools have grown only four million in the last twenty years, you can realize more clearly the real size of our task. Obviously, I am not saying that Southern Baptists will have the sole responsibility of reaching these eighty-one million new people, but *someone* must reach them, if they are to be reached at all.

Obviously, not every community shares alike in this explosive trend of our population increase, but thousands of communities are affected in a tremendous way. In practically every community—your community doubtless—there are increasing numbers of people to be reached, or there is yet a backlog of unreached people who claim the immediate attention of your church.

2. Urgency Grows

Our purpose in this chapter is to find motive and urgency for the work of our churches. Motive will come through a realization of the part your church plays in the total outreach of God's purpose and through a better picture of the unreached multitudes.

Were we to understand fully the worth of a soul, one lost person would suffice to stagger us with responsibility. But sometimes we can feel the urgency by considering the sheer weight of numbers. The following chart, provided by the Research and Statistics Department, Baptist Sunday School Board, is based on information secured from the United States Census Bureau.

U.S. POPULATION BY AGE GROUPS, 1959–1970

	Estimated Population 1959	Projected Population 1970	Population Increase
All ages	176,365,000	209,380,000	33,015,000
Under 4 years	15,966,647	18,755,576	2,788,929
4–5 years	7,766,784	8,734,343	967,559
6–8 years	11,276,703	12,687,766	1,411,063
9–12 years	14,031,282	16,369,523	2,338,241
13–16 years	11,373,823	15,916,596	4,542,773
17–24 years	18,212,761	28,571,196	10,358,435
25–34 years	22,843,000	24,946,000	2,103,000
35–up years	74,894,000	83,399,000	8,505,000

For every age group there is challenge and concern. Analyzing the foregoing chart, J. P. Edmunds says:

By 1970 there will be three million more children under four years of age than now; two and one-half million more Juniors; five million more Intermediates; eleven million more Young People; and eleven and one-half million more Adults than now.

"Bumper Crop"— Do we know what to do with our bumper crop of children any better than our wheat?

Notice how the increase of Young People between now and 1970 will almost equal the increase of Adults. That is because the avalanche of babies immediately following World War II will be reaching the Young People's age by 1970. In other words, the population is not stagnant. Like a tidal wave, it is constantly on the move, and gaining momentum as it moves.

3. *Population Makes Demands*

These demands are opportunities. They are also demands in terms of what our churches must do!

Not long ago a national magazine carried a graphic study of the population trends for the immediate years ahead with the intriguing title "Cash In on Who's Coming."

The "swells" in population were studied in relation to the markets they would produce and the effect they would have on business. The baby boom, beginning in 1943, brought immediate increase in demands for equipment, foods, toys, clothing, and other commodities for babies. As the annual "bumper crop" moved along, it has created demands at each stage—early childhood, school age, teen-agers. As the population boom moves up the scale, it will within the next few years double the number of potential college students. It will provide new investment and insurance opportunities, new jobs, new housing needs. As the bumper crop moves from one age group to the next, it will continue to create new demands for commodities and service. The children it will produce will bring another population explosion.

The business world studies such trends and prepares to meet them. Surely our churches must not lag behind business corporations in preparing for the people we must serve. In other chapters we will consider what such preparation requires.

IV. A Church's Contact with the Multitudes

God has given his churches both a message for the people and a method for reaching them.

1. A Church Has the Message and Mission

The plan of world redemption, conceived in God's own heart and made effective through God's Son, Jesus Christ our Saviour, is the profoundest revolution in human thought and conduct imaginable. All other revolutions known by man are insignificant by contrast.

What is the strategy of world redemption as given by our Lord? It is simply personal salvation—becoming a new creation in Christ—on the part of everyone who believes and accepts the free gift of God. "Therefore if any man be in Christ, he is a new creature: old things are passed away; behold, all things are become new" (2 Cor. 5:17).

Romans 10:9-10 declares: "If thou shalt confess with thy mouth the Lord Jesus, and shalt believe in thine heart that God hath raised him from the dead, thou shalt be saved. For with the heart man believeth unto righteousness; and with the mouth confession is made unto salvation."

To make possible man's salvation, Christ died. To put into operation the world plan of redemption, Christ established his church and outlined its work. Force would not be the method of world redemption. By precept and example, Jesus established the educational process—teaching and preaching —as the method by which men would be made aware of their need for regeneration and called to confront God's purpose for their lives. They must willingly accept the power of God working within them. By the means of teaching, preaching, and training, saved men are to be guided in their development toward full-grown Christians.

2. The Message Must Reach the People

Reaching people is the keystone ministry. Going after people—all the people—is the business of the churches. It was a great concern of our Lord. It occupied much of his thinking and was prominent in his instruction for the disciples. Even though he was forced at times to turn from the crowds, Jesus was always concerned about the lost multitudes. He placed them in the center of his program.

(1) *Reach them to teach them.*—Reaching people comes before teaching them. Early in God's dealings with his Chosen People, he instructed Moses: "Gather the people together, . . . that they may hear, and that they may learn, and fear the Lord your God, and observe to do . . ." (Deut. 31:12).

The purpose of the gathering was to teach the people. Instruction was and is desperately needed. The lament of the Old Testament prophets was that the "people are destroyed for lack of knowledge" (Hos. 4:6). They had turned deaf ears to their religious leaders. They were out of touch with God. They must be brought within hearing range.

(2) *Reach them to win them.*—Reaching and teaching people must come before winning them to Christ. It is logical and reasonable that the vast majority of those won to Christ each year are those who have been enlisted in Bible study through the Sunday school. In most churches 85 to 95 per cent of the baptisms come through the Sunday school. To be sure, revival meetings and special efforts of every organization in the churches make essential contributions; but the Sunday school is especially adapted to reaching, teaching, and winning the lost.

Recently I was in a church where an entire family—mother, father, and son—made public their profession of faith in Christ. It electrified the congregation. Back of this wonderful event was the effort of faithful Sunday school workers who had been working and praying for this family for five years.

(3) *Reach them to secure enlistment and development.*—Reaching people comes before enlisting them and guiding them in well-balanced Christian growth. Reaching them comes before stewardship and missions and dedicated Christian service.

Reaching people is not easy; it comes with great effort— concentrated effort. To the extent that Southern Baptists recognize the strategic importance of reaching people and are willing to concentrate on this phase of their work, great achievements will come.

In 1954 a Convention-wide effort to enrol people in the Sunday school was carried out under the theme "A Million More in '54." That year Southern Baptists showed twice as much gain in Sunday school enrolment as recorded in any previous year. This enrolment gain has contributed to growth in all phases of our work. Now it is time for another concentrated effort to get more people in Sunday school.

Reaching people is the concern of the whole church. Enrolling more people in Sunday school contributes to the enlarged service of every organization in the church. We can well afford to do what is necessary to keep our Sunday schools growing. We can ill afford to do anything that will hinder their growth.

V. What Shall We Do for the Multitudes?

Two inseparable questions confront every church as the time comes to evaluate achievements and prepare for future work. How many people shall we include in our ministry this year? How much will we do for their spiritual growth and development? To consider either question singly would be inadequate.

According to Ephesians 4, to "grow up" into Christ is the ultimate objective for every person redeemed by God's grace. Helping persons to grow and develop in Christian character and service is the ultimate work of a New Testament church. We must be increasingly concerned about the quality of our teaching and training, about our preaching ministry, about results that come in souls redeemed and in lives developed according to the pattern of Christ.

As Southern Baptists, we have been blessed in our efforts

to reach large numbers of people. Because of this we must be good stewards of our opportunities to teach, win, and develop those whom God has entrusted to us. With every additional person reached, our responsibility to teach becomes heavier. In fact, our ability to keep growing will be determined in large measure by the quality of work we do with those being reached.

The program of Sunday school work is, and must be, grounded in strong theological foundations and in sound understanding and teaching of the Scriptures, as well as in practical and progressive methods. Our Bible lesson courses and our training program for the preparation of Sunday school workers are dedicated to lifting the level of Bible teaching in our churches.

We need to give even greater emphasis to high quality work. Nothing short of our best is good enough. But let us keep the right balance between reaching and teaching. Let us covenant to extend our concern and our outreach to include all for whom we are responsible. At the same time, let every church continue to perform its divine mission of teaching and training for every available person.

WHAT WILL YOU DO?

Surely your reaction to this chapter will be a burdened heart, renewed prayer and dedication, and a deep determination to find out who and how many are the individuals for whom God holds your church responsible.

NOTE: Acknowledgment is made to *The Sunday School Builder* for permission to quote material used in this and other chapters.

CHAPTER 2

2

A Church Evaluating Its
School Sunday

THE CHURCH is the one institution, divinely ordained, given to men by which the kingdom of God comes in the earth. Jesus Christ (1) established his church; (2) set its purpose; (3) prescribed its functions; and (4) gave the Holy Spirit to guide and empower its work.

I. THE CHURCH DIVINELY INSTITUTED

The very foundation of every church and of every Christian is Jesus Christ himself. When believers understand that Jesus is the Head of the churches and the individual Christians in them, they will not falter in their assigned tasks. (See 1 Cor. 3:11; 1 Peter 2:5.)

1. Jesus Established His Church

Assuredly the church is of divine origin. The New Testament makes specific reference to it as "the church of God, which he hath purchased with his own blood" (Acts 20:28). "Christ also loved the church, and gave himself for it" (Eph. 5:25).

As J. Clyde Turner has pointed out, (1) a divine Architect planned it; (2) a divine Builder constructed it; (3) a divine Purchaser bought it; and (4) the divine Lord has commissioned it.[1]

[1] Turner, *The New Testament Doctrine of the Church* (Nashville: Convention Press, 1951), pp. 27–29.

17

2. *Jesus Set the Purpose of His Church*

There is no doubt as to what Jesus intended to be the purpose for his churches. They are to proclaim to all men everywhere the good news that Jesus Christ, through his death, burial, and resurrection, has provided the way to God. We have the word of Jesus: "Go ye into all the world, and preach the gospel to every creature. He that believeth and is baptized shall be saved" (Mark 16:15–16). We have the statement given through Paul: "God was in Christ, reconciling the world unto himself, not imputing their trespasses unto them; and hath committed unto us the word of reconciliation" (2 Cor. 5:19).

3. *Jesus Prescribed the Functions of His Church*

On the verge of his ascension, Jesus entrusted to his followers the responsibility for carrying on the work he had begun: "Go ye therefore, and teach all nations, baptizing them in the name of the Father, and of the Son, and of the Holy Ghost: teaching them to observe all things whatsoever I have commanded you: and, lo, I am with you alway, even unto the end of the world" (Matt. 28:19–20).

In this assignment we find the whole range of the task. In it we find preaching and worship; we find teaching and training; we find evangelizing, both at home and abroad. In it we find care for both the physical and the spiritual needs of men.

The church has a preaching function; likewise it has a teaching ministry. Either one without the other would not be effective. Teaching needs preaching. Without the declaration of the judgment of God upon sin and the glorious good news about salvation, the witness of our churches could easily tend toward moralism and legalism.

Preaching needs teaching to balance the ministry of the Word. Paul, in 1 Corinthians 12:28 and in Ephesians 4:11, makes it clear that the ministry of teaching is an essential part of the church's function. In this function the pastors must lead and direct. Those who are called to be teachers must take their places under the pastor's guidance.

4. *Jesus Gave the Holy Spirit to Empower and Guide in the Work of His Church*

Jesus accentuated the truth that the Holy Spirit is indispensable in the work of his church when he said that his followers were to wait for the promise of the Father. "But ye shall receive power, after that the Holy Ghost is come upon you: and ye shall be witnesses unto me both in Jerusalem, and in all Judaea, and in Samaria, and unto the uttermost part of the earth" (Acts 1:8).

II. ORGANIZATIONS IMPLEMENTING THE TASK

Why did Jesus Christ establish his church? Clearly, it was because he had in mind work for it to do. It was to become an instrument of conquest. It was to provide a fellowship and an atmosphere in which new converts would learn more perfectly the Word and would "grow in grace, and in the knowledge of our Lord and Saviour Jesus Christ" (2 Peter 3:18). It was to provide guidance in the practice of prayer and in the developing reality of Christ in the lives of its members. It was to be a fitting-out place where Christians would be equipped to carry out Christ's mission around the world.

Jesus did not spell out all the organizations that his church would need in every generation. Instead, he has left the Holy Spirit with his people to lead them in carrying out his assignment. Surely, God has guided through the years in setting into the churches those organizations through which they can effectively perform their ministry. Entirely in line with the assignment Christ has given, agencies or organizations in our churches have "come to the kingdom for such a time as this." Properly understood as agencies of the church, created, controlled, and directed by the church, these organizations become the legs and arms of the church in doing its work.

Thus has come the Sunday school with its Bible-teaching ministry, the Woman's Missionary Union with its missionary instruction and activities, the Training Union with its training in church membership, the Brotherhood with its ministry of enlisting men and boys in the work of the church, and the Music Ministry with its graded choirs offering channels of service in song to increasing numbers. To use these agencies properly, leaders must understand them as integral parts of the church. They are not different; they are, by assignment, the church at work in these several activities and functions. Dr. James L. Sullivan has said:

It is as foolish to think of a church accomplishing its task apart from the organizations as to expect a man to function properly physically without his arms or legs.

III. DISTINCTIVE CHURCH-BUILDING PURPOSES OF THE SUNDAY SCHOOL

Most of us grew up in Sunday school, no doubt! Perhaps, our very closeness to it is one reason why we need to look further into our understanding of it, and to get a good perspective of its distinctive place in the life of the church.

1. *Its Functions Are Comprehensive*

A good understanding of what a Sunday school is may be found by looking at its major functions: (1) It is a church agency; (2) its primal task is to teach the Bible; (3) its purpose is to win the lost to Christ and the saved to church membership and Christian growth; (4) it builds the preaching attendance; (5) it excels in the development of Christian character, Christian attitudes, and Christian practices; (6) it works effectively for Christian homes; (7) it unites the church members in the work of a church; (8) its opportunity is to enlist all the people in regular giving through the church budget; (9) its privilege is to enlist all the people in world missions; (10) its obligation is to reach all available people for all these blessings.

Through the years the following statement of definition has come to be quite generally accepted:

The Sunday school is an agency of the church led by church-elected, consecrated officers and teachers, organized for effective work and set to a fourfold task of (1) reaching the people, (2) teaching the Bible, (3) winning the lost, and (4) developing the saved through using the church members in effective service.

The Holy Spirit has outlined for us, through Paul, what is involved in our ministry: "He gave . . . pastors and teachers; for the perfecting of the saints, for the work of the ministry, for the edifying of the body of Christ: . . . that we . . . may grow up into him in all things, which is the head, even Christ" (Eph. 4:11–15).

The Sunday school has a vital part in all that is suggested

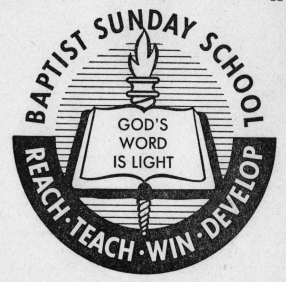

in this passage. The use of the Sunday school by Southern Baptist pastors through the years has confirmed the assertion of J. W. Jent:

Build a great Sunday school and the devil and all his cohorts cannot keep you from having a great church.

2. *Its Purposes Are Distinctive*

The nature, place, and purpose of a Sunday school fit it for distinctive and indispensable ministries in the fulfilment of the mission of a church.

The emblem of the Sunday School Department of the Baptist Sunday School Board portrays the truth that the Bible is the authority and the textbook for the teaching ministry of the church. It sets out four distinctive purposes: reach, teach, win, and develop.

(1) *Reaching the people.*—A Sunday school is a spearhead of advance that places the church in contact with the unreached masses. The message the church has, the gospel it preaches, the ministry it affords, are effective only insofar as the needy people are brought into contact with the church. The more than seven hundred thousand volunteer workers who serve as Sunday school officers and teachers are undoubtedly the most significant body of Christian servants to be found anywhere. Their first task is to reach the people, and no other agency or part of the church is so equipped to reach the unenlisted as is the Sunday school.

The formula found and applied by Southern Baptist Sunday schools is both simple and effective. There are five essential points that will guarantee to any church a continuous increase in the number of people reached and served:

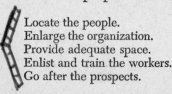

Locate the people.
Enlarge the organization.
Provide adequate space.
Enlist and train the workers.
Go after the prospects.

These essential factors, if properly applied, will build Sunday schools anywhere. They have contributed to the growth of churches in this land. As they are being applied in other countries, they prove effective there also.

The First Baptist Church in Sudbury, Ontario, Canada, invited some workers from the Sunday School Department of the Baptist Sunday School Board to share with them the Southern Baptist conception and plan of Sunday school work. This church decided to put the principles into operation. Within six months from the time the new program was inaugurated, the Sunday school had practically doubled in enrolment and attendance, and the pastor was rejoicing that there was new interest and enthusiasm for every phase of the church's work.

A church in a small town of less than one thousand population engaged in an enlargement campaign. Through a census they discovered 585 prospects. With an enrolment of 308 and total possibilities of 896, the church had at the beginning of the campaign only one department, 20 Sunday school classes, and a total of 28 workers. In a matter of a few months, a new educational building was constructed, and the school was fully departmentized, with multiple departments for some of the age groups. The organization included more than 80 officers and teachers, 40 classes, with an enrolment of 480 and an average attendance of 257.

In a metropolitan area a Sunday school had nine departments with some fifteen hundred enrolled and an average attendance of seven hundred. Department after department was added until, within a few years, there were sixty departments with twenty-eight hundred enrolled and an average attendance of seventeen hundred.

The Sunday school, by virtue of its organization, program, and purpose, provides the church with its greatest opportunity to reach the masses. A church may seem ever so strong in its quality of work done for those it has reached, but if the outreach is limited, then the ministry of that church is limited. In keeping with the spirit of Christ, outreach is a never-ceasing obligation of our churches.

Through a Sunday school that is constantly increasing its pattern of organization, the outreach of a church continues to grow, because the appeal of the Sunday school is to Christians and non-Christians, church members and nonmembers, young and old, from the cradle to the grave. A church through its Sunday school can provide for every member of every family in the community.

(2) *Teaching the Bible.*—Manifestly, other agencies of a church engage in a teaching ministry, but a distinctive function of the Sunday school is to offer a program of Bible study for every available individual. The pupils are graded for effective teaching; the buildings are planned with the same purpose in mind; the lesson materials are prepared to interpret God's Word on the ability level of every individual.

The program of training for Sunday school workers is directed toward the end of teaching the Word with power and effectiveness. The basic ministry of Bible teaching paves the way for the special ministries of every other church agency.

What Sunday school teachers are attempting to do is indeed significant. Their ministry has proved to be one of the positive forces to offset the flood tide of materialism, self-indulgence, and crime which incessantly threaten to engulf our land today.

J. Edgar Hoover, director of the Federal Bureau of Investigation, pays high tribute to the Sunday school as an effective crime deterrent. His constructive criticism is that the Sunday school simply is not reaching far enough. In general, those families and individuals whom it has not reached are responsible for the largest portion of the nation's annual crime bill.

Dr. James L. Sullivan says:

People need to know the Bible. It is God's Word and gives advice to men in successful living. It is the most necessary book on the bookshelf of humanity. If used aright, it will transform men and reform cities and nations. It is not enough, however, to teach about Christ. The teacher is to do his utmost to lead the pupil to Christ. Knowing Jesus in personal experience makes the truth of the Bible live and glow.

The late J. Percy Priest, congressman from Tennessee, said some years ago:

One of our great difficulties today arises from the fact that we are not spiritually conditioned for the place in history which destiny has decreed must be ours. . . .

Our scientific and technical progress has been so far-reaching that we have all but eliminated time and space insofar as our relations with the rest of the world are concerned.

While all of this was happening, we have fallen behind in our moral and spiritual development to the point that many thinking people wonder today whether man can be trusted with his own knowledge and devices.

To meet the desperate need of a strengthened and disciplined national character that is unwavering in the face of adversity, we must intensify our efforts in teaching individuals the Christian way. We must practice as well as proclaim the principles of the kingdom of God in every circle in which we move.

Our Sunday schools must assume the major share of the added emphasis on the teaching of individuals. . . . Each step forward in the development of one individual into a stronger Christian, and therefore a better citizen, adds that much strength to our national character.

Light is needed for all of us these days and every day. The increasing complexity of life, the tensions and problems of domestic and world relationships cause us to cry out for light and guidance from above, for "who is sufficient for these things?"

When has there been more unrest, fear, and uncertainty? When has there been more need for wisdom in the face of great learning than the leaders of the nations now experience? To help meet just such a need, the Sunday schools can function effectively today.

(3) *Winning the lost.*—The Sunday schools through the years have been very effective in evangelism. Many pastors testify to the fact that from 85 to 90 per cent of all baptisms come by way of the Sunday school.

Experience has proved that more people in Bible study means more souls won. In churches where the Sunday school enrolment is 50 per cent larger than the church membership, the ratio of baptisms to church membership is one to four. Where the Sunday school enrolment is equal to the church membership, the ratio is one to fifteen. Where the Sunday school enrolment is 20 to 30 per cent smaller than the church membership, the ratio is one to twenty-three. In churches where the Sunday school enrolment is even lower, the ratio of baptisms to church membership is much less favorable. How desperately, then, do we need to increase the enrolment of our Sunday schools in order that more souls may be won to Christ!

Many years ago Arthur Flake gave four reasons for considering the Sunday school as the chief evangelistic agency of the church: The lost people are found in the Sunday school; the taught people are there; those most susceptible to the gospel message are there; and the soul-winners of a church are there. Teaching the Word of God effectively prepares the way for soul-winning.

We have a strategy for winning multitudes of lost people. It is based on the discovery that a growing Sunday school means a greater evangelistic opportunity. The new people reached give us the best opportunity for evangelism. C. E. Autrey declares that assuredly the Sunday school is the most effective technique of the twentieth century for winning the multitudes of lost souls.

Enlargement, Bible teaching, and evangelism are inseparable elements in the work of a church. As G. S. Dobbins says so well:

Where Bible teaching precedes, evangelism has its richest harvest; and where Bible teaching follows, evangelism has its most permanent results.

(4) *Developing the saved.*—Christ's final words to the disciples (Matt. 28:19–20) underscore the balanced nature of the work of our churches. It consists of two major phases. One majors on teaching and making disciples; the other demands that those who are saved and baptized are to be taught to observe all of the things commanded by our Lord.

Is it true that often this note is missing when an invitation is given to make a public profession of faith in Christ? Do we give the greater emphasis to the acceptance of the Saviourhood of Christ and assume, perhaps with misplaced assurance, that faith in Christ is understood to include unreserved acceptance of the lordship of Christ?

Surely the teaching of the Word of God carries with it growth in the character, attitudes, thoughts, and actions of a Christ-centered personality.

Learning the lordship of Christ, however, does not come about merely through classroom teaching. There must be participation in service. Pupils need to engage in activities that will deepen the learning and make it a part of their lives. The Sunday school and Training Union are partners in the program. Those who are won to Christ must be trained and led into Christian service.

In the program of the Sunday school, a church has perhaps the greatest opportunity for putting its members to work. The Sunday school is the great employment agency of a church. It is possible to give every member of the church who is enrolled in Sunday school an effective place of service —as teacher, general or department officer, class officer, group leader, or as a member who is willing to visit and witness in the name of Christ.

There are two big reasons why all church members should help with the church program: The church needs to get the job done; they need the blessing of taking an active part in the work. As plans are made for enlarging and strengthening the work of your Sunday school, remember that putting people to work is an important part of your teaching program.

One of our finest churches, with a tremendous record of growth, has revealed one of its secrets: More than twelve hundred people have definite jobs in the Sunday school alone! Here is a major reason for the spirit of unity and spiritual growth which prevails.

IV. A CHURCH USING ITS SUNDAY SCHOOL

Of all the great contributions to Southern Baptists and the cause of Christ made by J. N. Barnette, perhaps the greatest is in his book *A Church Using Its Sunday School*. This book points up the basic difference between Southern Baptists and most other denominations in the expansion of their work: their concept of the Sunday school.

1. *Experience Has Positioned the Sunday School*

Where the Sunday school is not recognized and used, the pastor's opportunity to preach the Word of God is usually limited. Many Southern Baptist leaders who have visited other parts of the world report that the preaching in the Baptist churches there is not lacking in warmth nor in integrity to the doctrines of our faith. Yet, in most instances the churches are barely holding their own. In some cases they are even showing a loss. The reason lies in their concept of the Sunday school. Where the Sunday school is considered to be something separate and apart from the church and where it is made largely a means of teaching the children, it lacks the mature leadership to make it a force for building the church.

2. *Its Workers Make It Effective*

What a Sunday school can and will do for a church depends very much on the Sunday school officers and teachers—on their spirit, their dedication, their vision of their task, their preparation. It is their willingness to spend and be spent in the purpose to make Christ's love and compassion known, which either limits or extends the contributions the Sunday school may make.

3. *Leaders Attest Its Value*

The testimony of more than one hundred years of Southern Baptist history is that great churches are not built apart from great Sunday schools. M. E. Dodd, one of the great preachers of the past generation, said:

The Sunday school is the friend of childhood; the inspiration of youth; the strength of middle life; and the comfort of declining years.

The Sunday school has God's day for its time, God's house for its place, God's Book for its text, and God's glory for its aim.

The Sunday school is officered and taught by Christian men and women who are freely giving their time, talents, powers, and money to the end that the lost may be saved and the saved may be strengthened.

The Sunday school builds character, instructs the mind, warms the heart, feeds ambition, encourages the fainthearted, shields the tempted, and points the way of life for all.

The Sunday school deserves the sympathetic support, the prayerful interest, the loyal co-operation of every loving Christian, of every patriotic citizen, of every aspiring youth and every prattling child.

The Sunday school stretches out a friendly hand to one and all, old or young, and bids them enter into the Father's house and listen to the Father's voice as he speaks out of his holy Word.[4]

[4] Quoted by Arthur Flake, *Sunday School Officers and Their Work* (Nashville: Convention Press, 1923), p. v.

Arthur Flake, pioneer Southern Baptist Sunday school leader, gave us a clear understanding of the manifold functions of a Sunday school. He points out that the Sunday school can be used to teach the Bible, to gather needed information by a religious census, to extend the arm of the church into the community, to seek the unenlisted and unsaved, to train church members for service, to put church members to work as officers and teachers and class officers, to promote attendance at the worship services, to function as the chief soul-winning agency, to teach effectively stewardship and undergird the church's financial program, to provide guidance and an outlet for the social life of the members, to teach missions, and to provide a means through which to create and maintain denominational loyalty.[5]

Pastors throughout the length and breadth of the land indicate that the easiest, most logical, practical way to grow a great church is to concentrate on the use of the Sunday school in its ministry.

John H. Haldeman has said:

No one will doubt that the Holy Spirit has guided Southern Baptists as they have sought to devise a plan for carrying out Christ's command to teach. Through the years Southern Baptists have sought to improve and perfect this organization, which can most effectively teach the Word and lead into Christian service. From my study, observations, and experience has come this conception of the Sunday school.

The only successful way I have found to use the Sunday school is to believe that it is not just an organization of the church, but rather to consider that it is the church organized for the task of reaching people in order that they might be won to a saving faith in Christ and trained in a serving faith for the church.

This conception must become a deep conviction not only on the part of the pastor, but also on the part of the leaders of the church. To the extent that these leaders have this conviction and

[5] See Flake, *True Functions of the Sunday School* (Nashville: The Sunday School Board of the Southern Baptist Convention, 1930), chap. 1.

conception—to that extent will a church use the Sunday school in carrying out the command of Christ.

Thus the Sunday school becomes the church at the task of teaching what God commands us to know and do, and it furnishes opportunities for every member to have a place of responsibility in doing what our Lord has commanded. Here the church is organized to recognize the talents of each member, and the efforts of the people are marshaled into the militant work of the church and the kingdom of God.

V. A Church Building Its Calendar

Planning a church calendar is one of the most vital responsibilities of a pastor. What a church fails to get on the calendar generally fails to get done! Therefore, the process of planning the year's work, balancing the emphases, and getting the calendar set and adopted is of major importance.

Planning the calendar is a church function, usually carried out through the church council. The items in the calendar reflect what the church considers important. Sunday school activities should have a share of the time proportionate with their value.

It takes time for the essential Sunday school activities, such as planning meetings, census, enlisting and developing workers, training, perennial soul-winning, visitation, regular workers' meetings.

Timeliness is essential. There are seasons when certain activities are most needed and most fruitful.

A calendar must keep a balance of emphasis among the various interests of a church. From the abundance of activities suggested for the various organizations, leaders should select those most needed in their own situation. *Begin Here!*

VI. Testing the Worth of a Sunday School

The study provided in this chapter would suggest some ways by which pastor and others may test the Sunday school.

Pg. 10 Chart

1. *It Is Tested by Its Outreach*

The heart of God is turned toward people. Jesus our Saviour is eternally seeking people. Jesus loves the lost multitudes of people. The Holy Spirit yearns over the people. Our churches are set in the midst of the multitudes. What is our obligation? How far have we gone in reaching people? How inclusive is our concern?

2. *It Is Tested by Its Impact on the Community*

What a Sunday school does for those whom it reaches must always be a chief concern of the church. A functioning Sunday school also extends the influence of the church and helps to change the moral climate of the community in which it operates. There have been unnumbered instances in which the influence of a new Sunday school on a community has been evident in cleaner surroundings, more desirable recreational activities, reduction in crime, and other tangible changes. Changes in hearts soon lead to changes in environment.

3. *It Is Tested by the Spiritual Growth of Its Workers*

In a physical sense, the difference between life and death is growth. We either grow or die. Doctors tell us that our body cells are constantly dying, and if new cells did not grow to replace them, the body would die. Continuous growth, then, is a requisite to physical life.

In the spiritual life we are expected to grow also. In fact, spiritual growth is the only evidence of spiritual life. We are to "grow in grace, and in the knowledge of our Lord and Saviour Jesus Christ" (2 Peter 3:18).

What is expected of Christians generally, surely is required of a Christian worker—and to a greater degree, if possible. It is no light thing to be entrusted with the Word of God and with the spiritual care of the souls of men, women, boys, and girls. Every leader is called upon to be "an example of the believers, in word, in conversation, in charity, in spirit, in faith, in purity" (1 Tim. 4:12). He must take earnest heed of himself, must apply himself to reading, and must study, learn, and continue in the doctrine. Thus he can claim the promise, "Thou shalt both save thyself, and them that hear thee" (1 Tim. 4:16).

4. *It Is Tested by the Kind of Living It Produces*

The Christian program is one of growth—bringing the individual to a personal acceptance of Jesus as Saviour and Lord and on to maturity in Christ. Such an inclusive purpose is caught up in Paul's expression, "unto the measure of the stature of the fulness of Christ" (Eph. 4:13).

Peter's words also point the way of growth and effectiveness. We are given "exceeding great and precious promises" that enable us to partake of the divine nature. Besides all this we must add to our faith virtue, knowledge, temperance, patience, godliness, brotherly kindness, and charity. "For if these things be in you, and abound, they make you that ye shall neither be barren nor unfruitful in the knowledge of our Lord Jesus Christ." (See 2 Peter 1:4-8.)

J. O. Williams used to say so often that the program of our Sunday school "must be extensive enough to include everyone, must be intensive enough to enlist everyone, must be militant enough to challenge everyone, and must be spiritual enough to bless everyone."

WHAT WILL YOU DO?

As you test your Sunday school by the points suggested in this chapter, consider the achievements for which you can rejoice. How does your church measure up in its outreach in the light of the total number of its known possibilities? How does it measure up in comparison with the experience of churches cited in this chapter?

CHAPTER 3

A Church Discovering and Providing for the People

DURING the great depression of the 1930's, Inglewood Baptist Church in Nashville, Tennessee, was occupying a basement. The building program was at a standstill. The members were discouraged. Some were about to feel they would never get out of that basement. Then, one day someone put up a poster with the arresting caption, "How Far Can You See from Here?" The poster suggested: "Can you see a larger Sunday school? an adequate building? a greater church?" They could! A new spirit prevailed, and today Inglewood is a great and growing church with a beautiful building and one of the largest Sunday schools in the city.

How far can you see from where you are now? Is your church reaching as many people as it should? Is your Sunday school as large as it ought to be? What are your plans to make it grow? Have you started new departments and classes? Have you enough trained workers to do the job? Is your building adequate? Is your visitation program functioning? Have you set a definite goal for enlargement this year? Southern Baptists must keep growing to keep faith with the unreached multitudes.

The great tragedy of the ages is that the people are "scattered as sheep not having a shepherd." When Jesus saw the scattered multitudes, he was moved with compassion. The same motive in God's heart caused him to send his Son to seek and to save that which was lost. Finding the people must ever be a high priority concern of the churches.

I. DISCOVERING THE POTENTIAL OF YOUR SUNDAY SCHOOL

"Know your possibilities" might be a better way of saying it. Southern Baptist churches differ; and yet wherever they are found they are essentially the same in basic doctrinal beliefs and fundamentals of church polity. Some are in crowded, populous cities; others are in quiet villages or in the open country. Some are very large in membership; others are small. Actually, 40 per cent of Southern Baptist Sunday schools have an enrolment under one hundred; 70 per cent under two hundred; 80 per cent under three hundred; 86 per cent under four hundred, while only a relatively small percentage of our Sunday schools have an enrolment of one thousand or more. The churches that now are large, once were small. All these varied churches are alike in that they can reach more people than they are now reaching.

Here is a church that was thought to be dead, with only four living members left in the community. But was it dead? Could it live again? When an associational missionary went to this community and led in taking a religious census, possibilities for growth were discovered and new life came into that church. Within a year following the census, regular church services had been instituted again. A Sunday school, a Training Union, a Woman's Missionary Union had been organized. Sixteen persons had been received into church membership by letter, and forty had been baptized.

Here is a church in a great city. It started with limited facilities, few workers, and inadequate finances, but people were all around. The church considered the people, became concerned for the people, and began to provide for them. Within the space of a generation, this church has developed a Sunday school with an enrolment of more than twenty-eight hundred, has started four other churches whose Sunday school enrolment is nearly fifty-five hundred—a combined Sunday school enrolment of eighty-three hundred where only fifteen hundred were being reached a few years before!

Do you know the possibilities for your Sunday school? Have you located the prospects? The reach of your school will be limited until you do. The people are out there where Southern Baptists serve—millions of them unlisted! A share of them are in your community to be found and won. It is easy to find them, but they must be found!

When you find a prospect, you have taken the first long step in enlisting him for Bible study.

When you find a prospect, you are on the way to winning him to Christ.

When you find a prospect, you can make intelligent preparation for reaching him.

When you find a prospect, you can pray with more purpose.

When you find a prospect, you give more people an opportunity to help in enlisting him.

When you find a prospect, you open the way for love's conquest.

You find people by looking for them. What can you do to discover the potential of your Sunday school?

1. Start with the Church Members

Without doubt, every member of the church should be engaged in regular Bible study as an active participant in the Sunday school. Yet there are some four million Southern Baptist church members not now enrolled in Sunday school. This is an alarming condition. It is a matter of concern for every interest of our churches, because few church members who are not enrolled in Sunday school are active participants in any other part of the life and work of the church.

To discover your unenrolled church members, you will need two complete alphabetical rolls: the resident church membership roll and the Sunday school roll. Check the former against the latter and prepare a census card for each resident member not enrolled in Sunday school. You have an immediate, working list of prospects.

2. *Constantly Search for Prospects*

One measure of a good salesman is his awareness of prospects. Any business that is growing finds it necessary to add new customers. So it should be with our churches. Many different ways have been used effectively by churches in building up a prospect file.

(1) *Secure names of prospects from Sunday school members.*—Distribute census cards to every pupil enrolled in the Sunday school from the Junior age up. Ask that each one write the name, address, and approximate age of at least one prospective pupil he knows!

(2) *Find prospects from your Vacation Bible school records.*—Each year there are some 250,000 boys and girls in the Vacation Bible schools of Southern Baptist churches who are not members of any Sunday school. They provide a most responsive group of prospects. Additional hundreds of thousands of prospects may be discovered in the homes of these children, where there are fathers, mothers, brothers, and sisters not in Sunday school. Some of these unenrolled children, and their families, are the responsibility of your church.

(3) *List unenrolled members of families represented in Sunday school.*—A family file card will be valuable in revealing needed information about every member of the family. When the Sunday school has enrolled one or two members of a family, this is a good beginning for reaching the other members.

(4) *Secure information from public utility companies and business concerns.*—Many churches have found that, for a very small cost, utility companies will furnish them each

week with the names and addresses of all the families who have had meter changes or connections made. A follow-up will reveal accurate information regarding their church relationships. In many of the larger cities merchants have a "welcome service plan" in their approach to newcomers. Usually these merchants gladly co-operate with the churches by sharing the information gained.

(5) *Locate prospects from public school enrolment.*—State laws on the matter vary. However, in many communities superintendents and supervisors in the public schools are glad to help the churches in getting a religious information card made out by every pupil. It is both discouraging and challenging to discover what a high percentage of boys and girls in public schools are not active in Sunday school.

(6) *Use the visitors' cards in your worship services.*—This is a very effective way to secure names of good prospects for your Sunday schools. Many churches follow up this information immediately with a letter and/or personal visit from the pastor or some other member of the church.

(7) *Follow up on new church members.*—Perhaps most of those who join the church are already members of the Sunday school. If they are not, the best time to make an effective approach is right at the beginning of their new church relationship. Their names should immediately be placed on the prospect file and assigned to some department or class for visitation.

(8) *Continue an unrelenting search.*—There are many ways to find people if you keep looking for them! Ask the Cradle Roll and Extension department visitors to be alert for new prospects for all age groups. They move in areas that many other workers never touch. Encourage all Sunday school members in their regular visitation to take with them a supply of census cards and get information on any newcomers they discover. If you have salesmen, delivery men for

milk companies, and the like in your church membership, these can become effective sources of information about prospects.

3. Annually Make a Complete Religious Census

The census is the most thorough way for a church to discover its prospects. A good survey or census means an actual house-to-house canvass by consecrated workers who go afield in the interest of Christ and their church.

II. MAKING THE CENSUS EFFECTIVE

The census takers who go afield should know what information they want, why they want it, and how to get it. A thorough census rests on good preparation and efficient execution of plans.

1. Make Thorough Preparation

Let us consider some essential steps in getting people and properties ready for a census.

(1) *Positively present the values of a census.*—It secures names of prospects, names of lost people who need to be reached, and unaffiliated Baptists who need to be enlisted. It warms the hearts of the workers in the churches. It provides the needed motivation for enlargement and spiritual ministry.

(2) *Carefully select the date.*—It is good for a church to put in its calendar a definite date for an annual census. The Division of Evangelism of the Home Mission Board and the Sunday School Department of the Baptist Sunday School Board are co-operating in the effort to encourage every church to take its annual census, or survey, on the second Sunday in September. This date has the advantage of finding most of the people home from vacations. It will provide up-to-date information for the Sunday school and other church organizations for their enlargement and visitation emphases

at the beginning of the new year. A permanent prospect file, including evangelistic prospects, will make this information available for use throughout the year.

(3) *Accurately map the territory.*—In consultation with the pastors of the surrounding Baptist churches, determine the boundaries for the purposes of your survey. Secure or make a map that will show the streets and roads. Indicate the number of homes in each block. In rural areas mark the location of the houses on each road or lane. Divide the community into territories, each with about twenty families. Each such territory will require a census taker.

(4) *Prayerfully enlist the census takers.*—A census director should be secured who will handle the details of planning for and taking the census. At least one worker for each territory will be needed. If two can be provided, it will be better. Quotas for enlisting census takers may be set for officers and teachers in all departments and for Young People's and Adult classes. The Census Taker Enlistment Card, Form 695, is effective in securing commitments. Do not hesitate to ask people to help take a census. It is an opportunity for a vital Christian service and will be a blessing to anyone who gladly participates.

(5) *Promptly secure necessary materials.*—The needed supplies are available from your nearest Baptist Book Store. Order them well in advance of the census Sunday:

Enrolment Card, Form 20—Order in number about 10 per cent greater than the total present Sunday school enrolment, including the Cradle Roll and Extension departments.

Census Card, Form 675—This is the individual census card. Estimate the total number of family units in your territory and order at least five cards for every unit. Be sure to order enough.

Family Church Survey Record, (499-45855)—May be used instead of the individual census card. Order enough for every family unit in your church community (allow a few extra cards).

Census Assignment Envelope, Form 680—Order one envelope for each census taker (with a few extra).

Census Taker Enlistment Card, Form 695—Order 25 per cent more than the number of census takers needed.

Census Assignment Receipt Card, Form 700—Order one card for each census taker (with a few extras).

Prospect Visitation Assignment and Report, Form 120—Be sure you have enough to make an original and three copies for each prospect discovered.

(6) *Adequately prepare the community through publicity.*—Publicize plans for the census through the newspaper; get spot announcements on the radio; inform all the people of the plans. Such publicity will help to prepare for a good response to the census efforts.

2. *Execute the Plans with Dispatch*

Detailed plans for the religious census are given in the leaflet "Taking and Using a Religious Census." It sets forth the instructions to the census takers and gives guidance about making assignments, checking in the completed assignments, and following up the "not-at-home's." It also outlines the steps in preparing the information for use.

III. PREPARING THE INFORMATION FOR USE

Every time a census is taken, it should be used. Untold harm has been done when, for one reason or another, churches have engaged in taking a census and then have made little or no use of the information. The result is wasted effort, unclaimed opportunities, and a wall of discouragement against future participation in taking a census!

1. *Follow the Regular Procedure When Individual Cards Are Used*

Now that two types of census cards (individual and family) are available, it is necessary to make clear the procedure to follow in each case. The values of using the individual census cards and the steps in preparing the information for use are well known.

(1) Separate the cards, placing in Stack A those which indicate enrolment in some Sunday school. Put the rest in Stack B.

(2) From Stack B pull all cards that indicate preference for your church, no preference, or membership in a Baptist church outside the association. Study all cards for unsaved persons, even if preference is expressed for another church. If there is any question about the follow-up from the other church, hold the card until further visits have been made. Prospect cards for other Baptist churches in the association should be distributed to the respective churches. Cards for other denominations should be distributed or made available.

(3) Pull from Stack A all cards indicating members in your Sunday school. Alphabetize the cards and check against the alphabetized Sunday school roll. If there is discrepancy between a census card and the enrolment card, determine the accurate information, bring the enrolment card up to date or make out one, and destroy the census card. Any census card bearing a name not found on the Sunday school roll after this careful checking should be placed with the prospect cards.

(4) Combine and alphabetize prospect cards from the census and the church roll. If there are duplications, bring one card up to date and then destroy the other.

2. *Adjust the Procedure When Family Church Survey Record Is Used*

There is a family card available which, properly understood and used, can save time for both the census taker and the ones giving the information. The family card is valuable for the permanent files. The most reasonable way to get the needed information on the whole family is while the census or survey is being made in the home. For use in enlargement or visitation purposes, the information on the family card must be transferred to individual cards or slips.

G   Y   S   R   B

FAMILY CHURCH SURVEY RECORD

Family Name _____ House Number _____

Street Address _____ Telephone _____ Zone _____

Post Office _____ Date _____

Not Home ☐   Refused ☐   Vacant ☐   New Construction ☐

Do Not Write in Space	Given Name	Male	Female	Married	Member of What Sunday School?	Member of What Church? Where?	Are You A Christian?	Local Church Preference	Date of Birth			Age
									Month	Day	Year	

CODE 490–45655   BROADMAN SUPPLIES, NASHVILLE 3, TENN.   PTD. IN U.S.A.   (OVER)

(1) Check each name on the family card against the Sunday school roll. This is a simple matter when both are alphabetized. Use "S" on the family card beside the name to designate each individual found to be a member of your Sunday school. If a person claims to be on the roll and is not, check for possible error in the enrolment record and make an enrolment card if needed. If the error is on the census card, mark the name "P" on the family card, indicating prospect. Mark "P" against the name of every person who expresses preference for your school, no preference, or membership in a Baptist church outside the association. Mark with an "O" the names of those who indicate membership in another Sunday school or church or preference for a church other than yours. However, each unsaved person should be followed up even if he has family connection with another church. The pastor should check these special cases and determine which names to mark prospect.

(2) Make triplicate visitation assignment slips for all prospects marked on the family cards. Use Form 120, with

carbon. Keep the original and carbons of each slip clipped together. Make similar assignment slips for the church members not enrolled in Sunday school. Alphabetize and combine the two sets of slips, eliminating duplications.

In processing family church survey record forms, you have handled only prospect slips for your Sunday school. With one typing, you have slips which may be used as a permanent prospect file for the entire Sunday school, for each department, for each class, and an assignment slip for each prospect for immediate visitation by each department or class.

IV. Using the Information to Plan for Enlargement

The information you now have concerning prospects for your Sunday school will provide guidance in determining the number of new units and workers needed in order to reach and minister to the unreached.

1. *Grade the Information*

Before the information on prospects can be effective, either for visitation or as a basis for enlarging the organization, the cards must be separated by age groups and banded together, with the number in each age group indicated.

Cradle Roll ⎫
Nursery ⎬ Birth through 3
Beginner: 4, 5
Primary: 6, 7, 8
Junior: 9, 10, 11, 12
Intermediate: 13, 14, 15, 16
Young People: 17 through 24
Adults: 25 and above
Extension: All who cannot attend Sunday school

With this basic information you are now ready to make a careful study of what provisions have been made and what ought to be done to expand the organization. You are about to put faith into action.

STUDY YOUR SUNDAY SCHOOL POSSIBILITIES

Age Group	Recommended Maximum Enrolment (pupils)		1 Enrolled	2 Prospects	3 Total Possibilities	4 Depts. Have Now	5 Additional Depts. Needed	6 Total Depts. Needed	7 Groups or Classes Have Now	8 Additional Groups or Classes	9 Total Groups or Classes Needed	10 Workers Have Now	11 Additional Workers Needed	12 Total Workers Needed
	For a Dept.	For a Class or Group												
Cradle Roll	75	8												
Nursery	20	5												
Beginner	25	7												
Primary	30	7												
Junior	60	8												
Intermediate	75	10												
Young People-S	75	15												
Young People-M	75	20												
Adult	125	25												
Extension	75	8												
General Officers														
Totals														

2. *Study the Sunday School Possibilities*

By means of the chart facing this page it will be possible to develop a picture of what has been achieved in enrolment, study balance of provision for the various age groups, determine and recommend needed expansion, and indicate general improvement in the organizational pattern.

Please note that the figures in columns 2 and 3 are ceiling enrolments. They do not represent the recommended size for each unit. In the case of the Cradle Roll department, the figure in column 3 is the maximum number of homes per visitor.

Study the recommended maximum enrolments. Use the information in your Sunday school records to fill in columns 1, 4, 7, and 9. From your tabulation of the prospects discovered, fill in column 2. It is now a matter of arithmetic to complete the chart, thus drawing up on paper the kind of an organization your Sunday school needs to get the job done in the best possible way. In computing the number of workers needed, be sure to allow for department officers.

You stand now at a testing point, a Kadesh-barnea, in the life of your church. Faith dares to go on and claim the impossible in the name of the Lord. (Read Num. 13:30.)

V. Principles by Which a Sunday School Grows

Experience of Sunday school workers in all types of churches has revealed that certain principles produce Sunday school growth so consistently that they may be called laws of growth. In thinking about the dynamic development of the Sunday school, perhaps a review of these growth principles would be helpful:

Consistent growth is possible only through long-range and specific annual planning.

Consistent growth comes through a balanced provision for all age groups.

Consistent growth comes through a sound and solid motivation —evangelism.

A Sunday school reaches its maximum growth or "saturation point" according to its organizational pattern. To continue growing, it must move up the pattern from a class school to a department school, and from a department school to a multiple department school.

Classes normally reach their maximum growth within a few months after they are started. New classes must be started regularly if growth is to continue.

New classes (units) grow faster, reach more unsaved people, provide more workers, and stimulate growth and improvement in existing classes.

A church policy of discovering and assigning responsibilities for reaching the unreached is essential to growth.

Age-basis grading offers the most logical plan for starting new classes and assigning prospects for enlistment.

Promotion recognizes the natural laws of personal growth and development, and is essential to grading.

Classification on the age basis is essential to grading and promotion.

Classes with a narrow age range provide the best guarantee for reaching every individual for whom we are responsible, grow at a faster rate, and are easier to teach.

Sunday school enrolment is basic, and increases in proportion to the number of workers at a maximum ratio of ten to one.

Sunday school attendance is related to enrolment and is in direct proportion to the number of personal visits.

A Sunday school is limited by, and takes the shape of, the building it occupies.

Classes that meet individual spiritual needs through Bible study, Christian fellowship, and service opportunities grow consistently in enrolment and attendance.

Prepared and dedicated workers guarantee a growing Sunday school and assure permanent results.

VI. Making Room for Growth

Room for growth has to do with more than physical space, although certainly physical space is necessary for a growing

Sunday school. Sunday schools everywhere can grow. They can grow quickly when right provisions prevail.

Make room in heart and mind by discovering and knowing the possibilities for Sunday school enrolment in your community.

Make room in a physical sense by providing adequate space in your building for the unreached people in your community.

Make room by increasing the number of workers.

Make room by expanding the horizons, the vision, the abilities of Sunday school workers to meet the spiritual needs of pupils through thorough preparation.

Make room by sharing your interests, your enthusiasm, your blessings with the unreached through personal visitation.

WHAT WILL YOU DO?

This chapter has brought you face to face with some very challenging figures. Complete the chart "Study Your Sunday School Possibilities." Do the difficulties look mountain-high? Read Matthew 17:20. Underline the words "this mountain" and claim the promise.

CHAPTER 4

I. MORE WORKERS NEEDED
1. World Conditions Demand Christian Leaders
2. Continued Sunday School Growth Requires More Workers
3. Church Members Need to Work
4. Consider the Types of Workers Needed
5. Consider Where Workers Are Most Needed

II. QUALITY WORKERS DEMANDED
1. Requirements for Effective Leadership Are High
2. Self-Tests Are Revealing
3. Standards Must Be Set

III. SUFFICIENT WORKERS AVAILABLE
1. Pray for Workers
2. Recognize the Source of Workers
3. Work Through a Church Nominating Committee
4. List All Workers Needed
5. Study the Church Roll for Prospective Workers
6. Prayerfully Select the One Person Best Suited for Each Job
7. Confront the Prospective Workers with a Challenge
8. Make the Enlistment Task Easier by Reducing the Turnover of Workers

IV. TRAINED AND CONSECRATED WORKERS TO BE DEVELOPED
1. Specialized Training Is Needed
2. Make Use of the Church Study Course for Teaching and Training
3. Elect a Superintendent of Training
4. Enlist and Develop Study Course Teachers
5. Adopt a Challenging Program of Training
6. Recognize What Training Will Do

4

A Church Enlisting and Developing Sunday School Workers

JESUS recognized that workers are the essential element of success: "The harvest truly is plenteous, but the labourers are few; pray ye therefore the Lord of the harvest, that he will send forth labourers into his harvest" (Matt. 9:37-38). All that stands in the way of victory is the enlistment of an abundance of workers.

True, the statement just made oversimplifies the problem. However, it has the germ of truth needed by our churches today. A recent letter from a minister of education began something like this:

As you know, we are making an effort to get all of our people in training classes this year. As a result of this intensive training program our Sunday school attendance averaged 1,047 last month, whereas last year it was running between 700 and 750. There is nothing to take the place of finding and training workers.

Experience has demonstrated four concepts about Sunday school work: (1) More workers are needed. (2) Quality workers are demanded. (3) Adequate workers can be discovered and enlisted. (4) Trained and consecrated workers can be developed.

I. MORE WORKERS NEEDED

There are no limitations to the power of God, but he has restricted himself in his relationships with people. He has elected to bring about his will and way in the world through human instrumentality. People—leaders God can use—are

51

indispensable. The changing of individuals, of society, of world conditions is ultimately dependent on usable channels of personality.

1. *World Conditions Demand Christian Leaders*

In the long ago a message came to a pagan ruler: "Thou art weighed in the balances and found wanting."

Must we not believe that America, civilization itself, is no less in the balances today than was that vain, arrogant king of Daniel's time? We find ourselves confused and almost overwhelmed by the responsibilities of building a new world, of bringing discipline and order out of chaos, when we ourselves are so undisciplined.

All right-thinking men and women today are alarmed over the disintegrating influences of mounting divorces, increasing juvenile delinquency, and heavy consumption of liquor in our nation. Unchecked, these conditions will wreck us and bring our civilization crashing down upon our heads, even as sin has destroyed other nations.

What this world needs is the strong arm of Christian leadership. Whence will it come if not from our churches? The militant body of Sunday school officers and teachers and other workers must be greatly increased and the entire force rededicated to the work at hand.

2. *Continued Sunday School Growth Requires More Workers*

To try to reach the unreached people by loading more responsibility on the present Sunday school workers is to do it the hard way—or to find it impossible. Reaching more people follows when we put more trained workers in the field. It is just as simple as that. Success in the quest for more people hinges on additional workers. Jesus put his finger on the chief problem. The harvest is plenteous, the harvest is ripe, but too few workers have been enlisted to gather it.

The number of Sunday school officers and teachers should be doubled immediately in most cases. The pattern of organization should be increased. The class Sunday school should move up to a department Sunday school, the department Sunday school should move to a dual or multiple department school.

Southern Baptists have learned that in our Sunday schools we reach up to about ten people for every worker enlisted. If your enrolment in relation to workers has reached the ratio of ten to one, then your organization is full. You need more workers. Increase the number of workers until the ratio is about six to one, and your Sunday school will begin to grow again.

To illustrate: Here is a class of Junior boys with ten enrolled. That class is full. There are eleven prospects to be reached for that same age range. Find another teacher; give each teacher five of the enrolled boys and five or six prospects. Growth will be possible and almost certain.

The number of workers a church enlists actually sets the limit on the harvest that may be expected. What will you do in your church this year to provide needed workers to reach the multitudes?

3. *Church Members Need to Work*   *Less than 25% serve*

We are warned that the greatest threat to democracy is not enemies without, but indifferent friends within. Would we not have to agree that one of the most serious threats to our churches is the large number of nonfunctioning members? We have far too few of our members actively involved in the work of the churches. In the average church less than 25 per cent of the members are elected to any place of service. A minority of the members are carrying most of the burden. The work load is not equally distributed.

The multitudes need to be reached and Christians need to serve. In the Christian economy it is difficult to know which obligation comes first. The great harvest cannot be reaped without workers. Neither can any Christian develop to his fullest capabilities except through dedicated service. A functioning Sunday school provides the largest number of people with the most direct and effective avenue of Christian service that can be found in any church. Let us determine so to use the Sunday school.

4. Consider the Types of Workers Needed

In carrying out the work assigned to the Sunday school, there is ample opportunity for every type of talent Christians may possess.

(1) *Good administration is required for good work.*— Leaders must determine goals and objectives, set up adequate organization and resources to achieve the objectives, inspire and train workers for their tasks, guide in cooperative efforts, adopt standards of work, and evaluate results. The present size of the Sunday school, the planned size of the Sunday school, and the areas of responsibility for administrative officers determine the number of these workers needed.

Basic in almost any Sunday school organization are the pastor, the general superintendent, the department officers, teachers or visitors, and the class officers.

a. Pastor.—The pastor of the church is always the chief officer of the Sunday school. His leadership will be expressed through his conception of the place of the Sunday school; his guidance in the selection of officers and teachers; his assistance in securing adequate space, equipment, and materials; his prayerful support and encouragement of the worker. Certain phases of this responsibility may be assigned to other staff members.

b. Superintendent.—The superintendent is the elected administrative leader for the Sunday school. Certainly he will work under the direction of the church and in co-operation with the pastor. He shares in the work of every officer and teacher, providing all the resources at his command to help them do more effective work. In department schools, the superintendent will delegate many administrative responsibilities to the department superintendents.

c. *Associates.*—The superintendent will need one or more associates to help with specific areas of administration, training, and promotion. If one associate superintendent is adequate, he may be assigned a share of the responsibilities in whatever way seems best. Where there is more than one associate, each should be designated as superintendent of the particular area assigned to him.

The superintendent of enlargement works with the census, directs visitation, leads out in establishing new units, and works with the church missions committee in the establishment of new Sunday schools.

The superintendent of evangelism works closely with the pastor, encouraging full participation of the Sunday school officers and teachers in revival meetings and in sustained evangelistic efforts.

The superintendent of training plans the program of training opportunities and enlists workers in preparation for more effective service.

The superintendent of Standards leads in the interpretation, achievement, and maintenance of the Standards for the school, departments, classes, and groups.

The superintendent of audio-visual aids interprets and promotes the use of audio-visual aids in the teaching and training task of the Sunday school.

The classification officer is responsible for seeing that visitors and new members are assigned to the proper departments and classes and for enrolling new pupils.

The general secretary is responsible for securing accurate records on all departments and classes and for promoting the use of records in improving the work.

Where the church has a minister of education, he will, of course, work with the pastor in staff relationship and will provide guidance, encouragement, and assistance to the Sunday school superintendent and other officers and teachers in their assigned responsibilities.

(2) *Department officers, teachers, and elected visitors are needed.*—Even the smallest schools should have departments for at least five groups: Cradle Roll department, Extension department, Nursery departments, Beginner department, Primary department. Thousands of churches have departments for all age groups, and many have multiple departments in some or all age groups.

A general indication of need for each department organization is given by age groups. In small situations, some combination of duties may be needed.

CRADLE ROLL: A superintendent, associate superintendent, and visitors as needed (one for each district and every six to eight homes in the enrolment). A department may be organized with only one worker.

NURSERY DEPARTMENT: A superintendent for each Nursery department, with additional workers on the basis of one for every three to five children in the department. The smallest organization will require two workers.

BEGINNER DEPARTMENT: A superintendent, associate superintendent, secretary, and teachers on the basis of one teacher for every five to seven children enrolled

PRIMARY DEPARTMENT: A superintendent, associate superintendent, secretary, and a teacher for every five to seven children enrolled

JUNIOR DEPARTMENT: A superintendent, associate superintendent, secretary, a musician, and a teacher for each class (one for every six to eight boys or girls)

INTERMEDIATE DEPARTMENT: A superintendent, associate superintendent, secretary, song leader, pianist, and a teacher for every class (a class for every eight to ten boys or girls)

YOUNG PEOPLE'S DEPARTMENT: A superintendent, associate

superintendent, secretary, song leader, pianist, and a teacher for every class (one for every eight to fifteen men or women)

MARRIED YOUNG PEOPLE'S DEPARTMENT: A superintendent, associate superintendent, secretary, song leader, pianist, and a teacher for every class (one for every eight to twenty men or women)

YOUNG PEOPLE AWAY DEPARTMENT: A superintendent, associate superintendent, secretary, and a correspondent for every four or five members.

ADULT DEPARTMENT: A superintendent, associate superintendent, song leader, pianist, a teacher for each class (one for every ten to twenty-five men or women)

EXTENSION DEPARTMENT: A superintendent, associate superintendent, secretary, and visitors (one for every six to eight possibilities). A department may be organized with only one worker, the superintendent.

(3) *Class officers.*—A Junior or Intermediate class needs a president, vice-president, and secretary. (Nine-year Junior classes may substitute committees.) A Young People's or an Adult class needs a president, vice-president, secretary, and group leaders (one for every four to six members and prospects).

5. *Consider Where Workers Are Most Needed*

Increase is needed in all age groups! However, there are certain points where there seems to be the greatest immediate need for expansion and special emphasis.

(1) *Adults.*—Consider the vast number of adults in the community who should be members of the Sunday school. Measure this host by the fact that less than 40 per cent of the total Sunday school enrolment, including the general officers and members of the Extension department, are in the Adult age range. Is not something drastic needed to increase our enrolment of Adults?

We must reach Adults if we would maintain the continuous growth and health of our churches and if we would furnish needed leadership, example, and financial support for all phases of its work. Approximately four out of every nine Southern Baptist church members are not now enrolled in Sunday school. Most of these should be in Adult departments and classes.

The main reason why we have not reached more Adults is that we have not provided enough workers. In the smaller churches only about 10 per cent of the total Sunday school officers and teachers work in the Adult departments; in the larger churches 25 per cent. Yet more than half of the total possibilities for any Sunday school are in the Adult age range.

(2) *Young People.*—In general, churches have not made adequate provision for Young People. In some communities there are few young people. In others, there are great numbers concentrated in cities and in college centers. In every community there are some young people who need to be reached, taught, and won.

Aside from the Adult group, the average church is reaching a smaller percentage of its Young People than of any other age group. Every group of Young People needs adequate provision. The seventeen-year-olds need particular attention in separate classes and, where possible, in separate departments.

(3) *Intermediates.*—In the past ten to fifteen years great strides have been taken in enrolling Intermediates. In the Convention as a whole we now have enrolled about 85 per cent as many Intermediates as we have Juniors. Most churches should provide the same number of departments and classes for Intermediates as for Juniors. When such provision is made, a church may expect to hold in attendance those who are promoted from the Junior department and to enrol additional Intermediates.

(4) *Nursery children.*—The number of Nursery children

enrolled in Sunday school has skyrocketed in the past twelve to fifteen years. Any church that makes adequate provision for the children under four years of age will be gratified by the number of whole families reached. Few churches have yet made adequate Nursery provisions.

(5) *Cradle Roll, Extension, and Young People Away departments.*—These three departments minister to people who cannot attend the Sunday school. Through them a church can greatly expand the enrolment of its Sunday school and extend its ministry to individuals and areas otherwise untouched. Cradle Roll work will literally open the doors of homes to the full ministry of the Sunday school. The Extension department will make it possible for a Sunday school to reach every prospect for Bible study, even though he is unable to attend. The YPA department will permit a long-range contact with all Young People who are away from the community temporarily, either in the armed services or in college. Any Sunday school anywhere can maintain these three departments with abundant results.

II. Quality Workers Demanded *Amen!*

The longer one studies Sunday school work, the more he realizes that the basis for growth and improvement lies in what the workers really see in Sunday school. If Sunday school work appears to them as a small task and having little stature, then workers are not willing to give more than a margin of their time and strength to it. Pastors, superintendents, and ministers of education could scarcely find anything more important than to discover ways in which to lift the appreciation of workers for the opportunities and spiritual returns which their tasks afford.

1. *Requirements for Effective Leadership Are High*

We will not be able here to list all of the requirements. At best, the list will be partial and suggestive.

(1) *Commitment to Christ must be without reservations.*
—Halfheartedness is not in keeping with the demands of the
Christian life, much less with the responsibility of Christian
leadership. Thoughtful people today fear communism, not
because Communists are superior in intellect or strength,
but because there is a dedication to their cause. The world
will respect Christianity and churches to the degree that it
sees in Christians, and Christian leaders in particular, the
earnestness and abandon of dedication.

(2) *Loyalty in church membership must be unques-
tioned.*—The obligations of church membership must not be
taken lightly by anyone; workers have the added obligation
of example. The worker should be a member of the church
in which he serves, faithful in his attendance upon its services, active in its organizations, and hearty in his support of
the church in tithes and offerings.

(3) *Faith to accept responsibilities is in demand.*—
Leadership costs. It cannot be had until its obligations are
met. For that reason many fainthearted or easily satisfied
souls do not accept places of leadership. The Lord's work
needs the *right* leaders who, fully conscious of the implications, still have faith to accept the responsibilities.

(4) *Ability to make decisions must be cultivated.*—Decisions and complete commitments are hard to make. Often
they require unusual insight, unusual fortitude, and unusual
courage to follow through. Right decisions are not always
popular. Like Martin Luther, a true leader must make his
decisions born of conviction and be willing to say, "Here
stand I; God helping me I can do no other."

(5) *Aims must be concentrated.*—Any life is stronger by
concentration. A leader must devote his energies, interests,
time, and talents to his work if he is to lead others. Certainly,
one reason for the apostle Paul's power in his work was his
driving purpose: "This one thing I do."

(6) *Determination to get along with people must be sus-*

tained.—Not every worker has by nature a personality that adjusts well to others. However, every Christian can, through the power of the Holy Spirit, reflect the love of Christ in all his relationship without others.

(7) *Faithfulness to the heavenly vision must be maintained.*—Perhaps a chief weakness of human nature is to become discouraged easily in the face of increasing problems— to forget the high resolves of the heart made when the vision was bright. A leader must maintain his vision and faithfully pursue it to ultimate realization. Like Paul, he must be able to say, "I was not disobedient to the heavenly vision."

2. *Self-Tests Are Revealing* Read in Class!

Christian workers should seek for success. God wants us to succeed. His grace and resources are at our disposal. Truly the key to happiness and success in Christian service lies in us. Will you explore some questions that may help you discover that key?

(1) *Am I confidently in the center of God's will?*—No one can achieve happiness unless he is convinced that he is where God wants him to be. Have I accepted my place of service for any other reason than that I feel God led me to it? When I know I am where God wants me to serve, then I can claim with assurance every resource of God to strengthen me for our task.

(2) *Do I have the right conception of the task?*—A leader grows in his ability as he grows in his conception of his work. "Walk worthy of the vocation wherewith ye are called" (Eph. 4:1).

Not only does a high evaluation of my work call for noble living, but it challenges my best at all times. I have the opportunity of sharing my life, my ideals, my aspirations, and my insight into the Word of God with boys and girls or men or women. Where could I hope to make a greater investment? In the lives of these individuals, I have the privilege of helping to change doubt to faith, resentment to appreciation, rebellion to obedience, self-will to dedication, frustration to a satisfying life in Christ.

(3) *Do I take the necessary time to grow into deeper experiences with God?*—The joy and effectiveness of a Christian worker come through sharing with others. I am constantly giving out, and if I am to continue to share helpfully, I must continue to feed my own soul.

Am I making worship pre-eminent in my life? My busy, crowded life of constant activity, even of Christian service, can crowd out that which I desperately need. I must "grow in grace, and in the knowledge of our Lord and Saviour Jesus Christ" (2 Peter 3:18).

(4) *Do I seek constantly to develop the characteristics required for Christian service?*—To be happy in Christian service requires working at the job of becoming the kind of person required for a good leader.

3. Standards Must Be Set

Leadership is determined by the type of program the church is set to promote. As Christian leaders, we share the purpose of Christ: "For the Son of man is come to seek and to save that which was lost" (Luke 19:10). This special purpose requires leaders with special characteristics.

The Christian leader must be a convinced person. Not a little of his own spirit and conviction is caught by those who follow. One must know the reality of God and the worth of the cause he represents.

A Christian leader must be a sensitive person (not a selfish person), alert to the needs of people. It is ours to teach and to win and to conserve human personality, and effectively dealing with persons can never become a professional matter.

A Christian worker must be a properly motivated person, who sees Christian leadership as a calling, a fellowship with

God in the service of guiding growing life. The dedicated leader will be willing to study and prepare and train and work in harmony with others for the achievement of his task. He will gladly take advantage of every training opportunity which his church affords him and which he may gain through his conferences and contacts with other workers.

Sunday school officers and teachers are volunteer workers. Being volunteer workers should not, however, reduce the level of service; perhaps it should bring forth even a higher degree of performance. During wartime, the especially dangerous assignments are usually awarded to volunteers!

Determining the right kind of standards for the officers and teachers is a serious matter. It is something that should not be imposed upon workers—indeed it cannot be imposed successfully. Perhaps a properly prepared covenant could be worked out mutually by the workers and adopted by your church as a challenge to those who accept places of responsibility in the Sunday school.

The Sunday School Board publishes a worker's covenant that might be helpful in this respect. Copies may be secured for each worker at a nominal cost through the nearest Baptist Book Store. Many churches, of course, prefer to work out their own.

III. SUFFICIENT WORKERS AVAILABLE

God will place in every church enough workers to do the work of that church. Every pastor who has wholeheartedly accepted that fact has found it to be literally true. The workers have to be discovered; they must be enlisted; they need to be trained. But they are there and they will respond. Here is the point at which to exercise faith. The miracle of all the ages is God's ability to accomplish his work through plain people.

1. *Pray for Workers*

Reaching lost people is God's concern. Leading to abundant living is Christ's purpose. Sharing in this work is the commission of our churches and of every Christian.

Since it is the Father's concern, Jesus tells us to pray to the Father. Since workers are necessary to accomplish the work, we are to pray for workers. Since such prayer will grow out of and lead to a deepened concern for the multitudes, Jesus commands us to pray to the Father for workers.

2. *Recognize the Source of Workers*

Workers will be found—must be found—right in your church membership. That is the only source you have. You will find workers by looking for them, not by overlooking them. Someone has said that workers will be found in the crowds, not in the clouds. Too often leaders have looked right past the ones who have been faithful in attendance through the years and have never really considered them as possibilities for service. Many people are not at work simply because they have not been asked.

3. *Work Through a Church Nominating Committee*

In an effort to lift the level of all their workers, churches are discovering that a church nominating committee functioning throughout the year is most effective. This committee is authorized by the church to select individuals for places of service.

The committee's relationship to the Sunday school will be definite and effective. It does not reduce the superintendent's sense of responsibility; it helps him screen the workers and thus avoid the confusion and frustration of various independent approaches to individuals. The committee should select and enlist the general superintendent first and recommend him to the church for election, by the first of June or earlier, if possible. After his election, he will serve with the committee to consider the other Sunday school officers and teachers.

The nominating committee may approach the suggested worker directly to secure his agreement to serve. However, many churches prefer to let the committee instruct the Sunday school superintendent to take the lead in approaching proposed Sunday school workers. In any event, all names will be cleared with this committee before any persons are contacted.

4. *List All Workers Needed.* ~~ask Jake to do this !~~

The entire Sunday school organization should be reviewed as nominations are considered. A helpful plan is to use the chart "Study Your Sunday School Possibilities" given in chapter 3. List all the present units, the new units to be added, and the total number workers required. Decide on the present workers who should be re-elected. Compile a list of all the vacancies. Thus, the committee will have a list of all places of service to be filled in the entire Sunday school organization.

5. *Study the Church Roll for Prospective Workers*

The list of positions to be filled makes it possible to pray specifically for the Holy Spirit's guidance in discovering workers. Study the church roll, noting every person who is not already in service. Ask only two questions about him: (1) Is this person morally and spiritually fit? (2) Could he do the work if he would? If the answer is yes, consider him for the position. Do not ask at this point how much experience the person has had or how much training he has. That can be taken care of later.

6. *Prayerfully Select the One Person Best Suited for Each Job*

Members of the committee will seek to be very conscious of the guidance of the Holy Spirit. Definite information as to the particular requirements of each job should be kept in mind as each person is prayerfully considered. As the individual is approached, there will be added force when the committee can say: "We believe you are the best person available for this job. You are the only one under consideration, and we feel led of the Holy Spirit to approach you."

7. *Confront the Prospective Workers with a Challenge*

The way individuals are approached for places of service has much to do with their acceptance. Make the approach a matter of prayer. Make the approach personal. Make an appointment for a personal conference. Be prepared with information about the opportunities and responsibilities which go with the position. Magnify the opportunity to serve. Emphasize both the joys and the responsibilities. The "Oh, it won't take too much time" approach is not the way to get topflight workers.

8. *Make the Enlistment Task Easier by Reducing the Turnover of Workers*

The average Sunday school has a turnover of approximately 30 per cent in officers and teachers each year. Some terminations are necessary. However, through training, good equipment, genuine appreciation and encouragement, and high standards of achievement, a church can secure more effective workers and thus forestall resignations.

IV. TRAINED AND CONSECRATED WORKERS TO BE DEVELOPED

A pastor related a truly remarkable experience. Two years before, the church had launched an intensive program of training which, he indicated, had been largely responsible for the growth of the church. In two years they had gone from 37 workers in the Sunday school to 157, from a Sunday school enrolment of 150 to an enrolment of 1,127; from 7 departments to 27. The church had been in two building campaigns and had started two missions, both of them staffed by workers from the mother church.

What had been back of this unusual development? The church had offered its workers 68 different training opportunities during the year, and a total of 1,173 awards had been earned. During the previous year three of the workers had been to Glorieta Assembly, and the church voted $1,500 to send all of the department superintendents who could go the following year.

1. Specialized Training Is Needed

Since Sunday school workers are volunteer workers, most of them have had little formal training for the task of teaching or of administering the program of Bible teaching. Their willingness to serve must be matched by the church's willingness to provide the special help needed.

(1) *The administration of a Sunday school is exacting.*— In many communities the Baptist Sunday schools have an aggregate number of workers larger than the faculty of the whole public school system. Certainly the importance of their work is as great and greater. Laymen who are responsible for Sunday school administration need guidance and opportunities for growth on the job.

(2) *Sunday school teaching demands the best preparation possible.*—Teachers must know the Word of God. They must know the program of their church and denomination. They must know the needs, interests, and abilities of their pupils. They must know how to communicate effectively the truth of God's Word to those they teach.

Even persons who are well trained in their professional

pursuits need the special training their churches can give them for the task at hand.

2. Make Use of the Church Study Course for Teaching and Training

On October 1, 1959, a new course came into existence. It is a blending of the Sunday School Training Course, the Graded Training Union Study Course, and the Church Music Study Course. Awards previously earned in any of these courses may be transferred to the present course. The Church Study Course for Teaching and Training is an instrument for the use of the churches to indoctrinate, train, and develop all the people for fuller participation in all the program. It is comprehensive in content, providing books in nineteen categories; it is graded; it is church centered; and it has one system of awards. Sunday school workers are interested in the whole course, and credits earned in any category may be applied somewhere to the diplomas offered. Category 17, Sunday School Principles and Methods, is especially significant for Sunday school officers and teachers. Full details may be found in the free catalog *Church Study Course for Teaching and Training*.

3. Elect a Superintendent of Training

One of the most competent persons in the church should be elected as a Sunday school officer responsible for supervising and promoting the training of the workers and potential workers. Among his duties would be to—

Lead in planning an annual Sunday school training program.

Promote the training program.

Be responsible for detailed handling of training opportunities sponsored by the Sunday school, such as Bible Study Week, Preparation Week, Operation Home Study, and Bible Survey Plan. For these events it would be his responsibility to secure teachers, order study course books, and to request awards.

Maintain individual record of awards, unless some other person has been named for the job. It is recommended, however, that a Church Study Course Records secretary be elected for this work.

Give special attention to books in category 17, working with all the departments to see that every year all officers and teachers receive the basic training needed.

4. *Enlist and Develop Study Course Teachers*

While it is desirable for a pastor or for a minister of education to teach many of the courses, other leaders in the church should also be developed. Some churches, by providing two-hour sessions each week arranged at convenient hours, offer as many as a hundred or more training opportunities per year. To maintain these courses requires an abundance of competent teachers. It would be well to select potential study course teachers and give them opportunity for study at Ridgecrest, Glorieta, clinics, and workshops.

5. *Adopt a Challenging Program of Training*

Training opportunities should be provided around the calendar. Sunday school Preparation Week in September promotes the study of a general administration book and serves to project the Sunday school program for the coming year.

Bible Survey Plan logically can begin in October, but it may be started any time during the year and continued with two-hour class sessions each week for approximately eight months.

Bible Study Week in January offers the entire church the privilege of studying a specific Bible book or theme.

Vacation Bible school training opportunities come particularly from February to May. They should include a study of *Better Vacation Bible Schools* and the five Vacation Bible school textbooks for the particular year.

Operation Home Study comes during the summer months from June through August. It promotes the study of a recommended book by the individual method. It is aimed to reach all Sunday school workers, including Adult and Young People's class officers.

Association group schools and central training schools are offered in many associations during October and at other times of the year. Thousands of officers and teachers are thus provided an opportunity to study their age-group books under competent leadership, while it would not be feasible to provide age-group classes in their own churches.

Every month of the year is a good time to get training done. John Haldeman, pastor of Allapattah Baptist Church in Miami, has said that once he thought his people were too busy to have more than one training opportunity a year. He has come to realize that they are far too busy for just one training opportunity. A number of opportunities make it possible for every member to have some training.

6. *Recognize What Training Will Do*

The values of a good training program have been amply demonstrated by churches of all types and in varying circumstances. Sunday school workers with a minimum of formal education have become highly proficient in their service through the study and application of information in study course books. Workers who have had the best of education in the secular field and even those who have had the benefit of seminary courses find that they need to keep abreast of Sunday school methods through participation in a training program. A good balance is maintained when the study of books is co-ordinated with an in-service training program of a workshop type, carried out through the weekly officers and teachers' meetings.

A training program will help to—

- Change the haze of indifference and complacency into a blaze of enthusiasm and concern.

- Convert indefinite objectives into a moving, gripping purpose.

- Make pastors and superintendents to see workers "that aren't there."

- Change conditions from the way they are to the way they ought to be.

- Reveal to the leaders possibilities they had not dreamed of.

- Lay stable foundations in the church for permanent progress.

The road to Sunday school success is paved with the solid stones of preparation and training.

WHAT WILL YOU DO?

This chapter is a call to every teacher of Adults or older Young People to search his class for members who need to go out in service and to enlist these members in a training program. It should also lead to personal commitment by every worker to a full program of training.

CHAPTER 5

A Church Breaking Through the
Space Barrier

BRUCE BARTON popularized a phrase some years ago, "When you are through changing, you are through!" Southern Baptists say, "When you are through building, you are through!"

A large department store in a Southern city has taken as its slogan: "The Store That Will Never Know Completion." During these recent years it has lived up to that slogan by constantly increasing and adjusting the space to provide for more business. So it is with our growing churches.

A letter came stating:

We moved into our building on March 9, the first time the church has ever had an educational building. The Juniors were meeting in the downtown theatre, the Intermediates in the Masonic building, and Adult classes were meeting in a Building and Loan office. It is good to have them all under one roof.

Six years before, the enrolment of that Sunday school was 178, with an average attendance of 129. At the time the letter was written, the enrolment was 1,226, or a net gain of 1,048 in five years. Back of this growth was a move-up from seven departments to twenty-five departments and from 20 workers to 153 workers.

The church entered the new educational building in March. A study of the enrolment and attendance figures for the preceding five years tells a significant story. Increased units and temporary space quickly enlarged the enrolment and attendance. Then saturation set in, and growth was retarded until the new building gave a fresh thrust to the outreach.

	1953	1954	1955	1956	1957	1958
Enrolment	178	363	625	926	958	1,057
Average Attendance	123	292	431	481	521	781

I. Seeing the Significance of Space

There are two statements often made which set out the basic Southern Baptist philosophy regarding church buildings and their relationship to the total program: Space holds the key. The buildings set the pattern.

Many factors are involved in Sunday school enrolment gains. Unquestionably, there is high correlation between space provided and Sunday school growth. Two things we must remember about the provision of space. First, it is impossible to reach more people than the building can hold. Second, it is impossible to keep the attendance up to the maximum capacity of the building all the time. Like a hotel, a Sunday school can hardly maintain 100 per cent occupancy. (It must be said, however, that some churches are doing a magnificent job of proving the exception to those two statements!)

1. Build for the Baptist Program

Not all architects know how to plan a building adequate for Baptist use. Our church houses should be beautiful. They should be well constructed. They should be commodious. But a church building may have all these desirable qualities and not fulfil the needs of a Baptist church. Building for the Baptist program is an inclusive and distinct concept. W. A. Harrell, secretary of the Church Architecture Department of the Baptist Sunday School Board, has well said:

The houses that churches build speak for the entire philosophy, planning, and thinking of the church. The conception that the church has of its position and task is expressed in the house that it builds.

(1) *Build for a total constituency.*—The concept of provision for total constituency is at the heart of planning for the ultimate space needed. It means that we expect to reach all ages in the church program. It means providing for the little children in the Nursery departments. It means providing for the various age ranges of Adults. It means increasing facilities at all points between!

(2) *Arrange the space for best teaching and continuous growth.*—Space alone is not enough. Even well-appointed, elegant space is not the point. The sizes and arrangements of the rooms must be in keeping with the teaching procedures and adaptable to Sunday school enlargement patterns.

(3) *Give priority to educational space.*—In most instances the first units to be provided should be educational space— even when the church auditorium is inadequate. There are sound reasons for this claim. Educational space makes possible a growing Sunday school. Through a growing Sunday school the church will increase in membership and in financial strength. Thus, an adequate auditorium can be built sooner and with greater ease if educational space comes first. Also, this plan provides time for a church to determine its growth potential and to plan an auditorium large enough for its needs.

(4) *Make long-range plans for construction by units.*— This is the common-sense approach to providing space. Few churches are able at one time to build a complete and adequate church house with auditorium and educational facilities. By carefully planning what the ultimate building is to be, a church can build one unit which may be immediately adapted to the complete church program, yet fit into the over-all pattern for expansion. Then other units may be added one by one, with necessary readjustments, until the final plan is complete.

2. *Continue Building for Continued Growth*

Someone has well said that a church will never grow to need the facilities it fails to provide. It is easy for a church to limit its own future by failing to continue to build. James S. Riley has said:

The sobering fact is that failure to plan proper buildings for a church program is to sacrifice the future of the church on the altar of thoughtlessness. A church apparently may thrive on spirit alone and for a brief time make phenomenal records of achievement. A day of reckoning is inevitable, however, unless proper steps are taken to conserve these gains. Deliberate reasoning dictates that adequate buildings are indispensable if a church is to continue beyond the first generation as a thriving and effective New Testament church.

(1) *The experience of smaller churches proves that buildings build.*—It is the same everywhere. Large churches, and all in between have found that they can grow and continue to grow if they have the vision and devotion to make adequate provisions in leadership and facilities.

Here was a Sunday school with an attendance of 39. The superintendent and pastor led out in a program of training for their people. Desire was created for a better school. The study led to prayer, planning, and a greater compassion for the lost people all around. Then came grading, establishing more classes, providing for Nursery children, setting up Extension and Cradle Roll departments.

The building became crowded; attendance leveled off. Fortunately new vision had gone to work, a new educational building was constructed, and the church continued to grow. In four years' time this rural church had grown from a church membership of 73 to 159, from a Sunday school attendance of 63 to 122. The latest word from the church was, "We moved into a new building and are now having to build another building, because growth has exceeded expectations." The superintendent added, "Where there is vision *fewer* people perish."

(2) *The experience of larger churches proves that buildings build.*—Some time ago Rowland E. Crowder, consultant in the Church Architecture Department, Baptist Sunday School Board, made a survey of the ten largest Southern Baptist Sunday schools. It was extremely interesting to discover the almost identical experience in these churches throughout their history, some of them for over a hundred years. There was little growth in enrolment until a major building program made possible an enlarged organization. A spurt of growth followed. Soon saturation set in and a need for new space arose. Again a building program brought growth. So it continued through departmentization of the Sunday schools and on to the multiple departments. Each of these ten largest Sunday schools has engaged in from five to eight major building programs in its history. Dr. Crowder concludes: "The churches with building programs that will never know completion are the ones that will continue to grow and win multitudes for the Lord."

TEN LARGEST SUNDAY SCHOOLS

Church	Sunday School Enrolment * (1958)	Major Building Programs
First, Dallas, Texas	7,320	6
First, Lubbock, Texas	5,576	8
First, Amarillo, Texas	4,887	7
Bellevue, Memphis, Tennessee	4,481	5
Cliff Temple, Dallas, Texas	4,226	6
First, Charlotte, North Carolina	4,117	7
First, Tulsa, Oklahoma	4,103	7
First, Wichita Falls, Texas	4,102	5
First, San Antonio, Texas	4,095	6
First, Oklahoma City, Oklahoma	3,864	6

* From statistical tables in *The Quarterly Review*, XVIII, No. 4 (1958), pp. 23-76.

II. Providing Needed Space

With all of the tremendous building of church houses done by Baptists in these recent years, we still have not kept up with the need. In most instances providing space will certainly require building, but there are other matters that need careful consideration.

1. *Achieve Proper Attitudes About Space*

Perhaps most of our problems will be solved when we can lead our people to put need first and let the necessary steps to securing space follow. A recognition of need properly presented will usually get desired results—even to the point of having an Adult Bible class volunteer its space for a new Nursery department! Consider some of the needed attitudes about space.

(1) *Realize that all the space is for all the church.*—If there are those in your church who do not have that attitude, it creates needless confusion and also results in wasted space that could have other uses. Let all of our classes, departments, and groups recognize that all of the space belongs to the church and is for the uses the church sees fit to make of it. Think of the total church program.

(2) *Evaluate the use of space annually.*—At least once a year (more often in fast-growing situations) it is well to make a careful study of the enrolment, attendance, and prospects for each of the departments and classes and to examine the space these units now occupy to see if any re-adjustment should be made.

(3) *Develop the ability to see space.*—Perhaps this seems to be a strange statement, but it is quite true that church workers have lived with their present arrangements so long that it simply does not occur to them that adjustments could be made or that there are unused areas that could be put to service.

(4) *Invite someone to help you look for space.*—Here again this may seem to be a simple and unnecessary observation. However, a Sunday school worker from the state office or from the Sunday School Board, or a pastor or worker from a neighboring church, studying your situation with you may find space that could be pressed into service—space that you, perhaps, have overlooked. Try it! You may be too close to your own situation to get off and study it with perspective.

In more than twenty-five years in work with churches throughout our Convention territory, I have visited many churches that have believed their buildings were full, yet at least 80 to 90 per cent of these had some undiscovered space where they could start more units. Unused space may be found in offices, kitchens, hallways, church auditoriums, balconies, dining areas, assembly rooms, stages, platforms, choir lofts, furnace rooms, baptismal dressing rooms, foyer.

2. Get Maximum Use of Available Space

It is quite possible and usually true that there is wasted space in a crowded building. What can be done to correct this situation if it exists in your church?

(1) *Shift units to provide maximum usage.*—We have just indicated that an annual study and evaluation of the use of space should be made. The assignment of rooms should not be considered so inflexible as to permit some department that has been unable to fill the space for an entire year to continue to occupy it when some other unit needs it or when a new unit should be started.

(2) *Rearrange and remodel space*—By removing or adding partitions, changing doors, including hallway space, rerouting traffic, and making other adjustments, it is often possible to improve the use of your present space, at least as a temporary measure.

(3) *Use the same space twice.*—Here, indeed, is a sug-

gestion that needs careful examination. The plan would never be suggested except as a temporary measure and as a last resort!

Some churches, however, have discovered that when their growth is so great that they cannot build fast enough, they can provide for two Sunday school sessions—one before the preaching service and one after. In some cases, where the auditorium is inadequate, there would also be two worship services. There are obvious disadvantages to this plan, and most of the churches that have used it have secured added space as quickly as possible so as to have all of their people together in the same schedule.

(4) *Keep units small to make effective use of present space.*—Smaller units are better from the educational viewpoint—and from a practical viewpoint as well! It is always easier to find an area which would permit a small department or class being added than it is to find a larger area.

3. *Use Space You Do Not Have*

The reference is to space that you do not have, but can get. There are several ways to do this.

(1) *Buy or rent buildings nearby the church.*—Many churches have discovered that this is the most economical and easiest way to solve their space problems. If adjacent property is available for purchase, it is always worth more to the church than it is to anyone else, provided your church needs it for expansion. Even if the buildings are not good, the land is always valuable. But in many instances the buildings can be remodeled at nominal cost and pressed into service.

Some time ago Wayne Dehoney, then pastor of Central Park Baptist Church, Birmingham, Alabama, underscored a basic philosophy about growth, new units, and space, which his own experience amply illustrated:

Southern Baptist churches have grown numerically, only as

we have discovered how to efficiently use the Sunday school as our major enlistment agency.

A graded, small-unit, multiple-unit school sets the pattern for growing a great church.

A Baptist church can in from nine to eighteen months fill with people any space that it will provide, and these new people, filling this new space, will bring in new money that will pay for this new space in from three to five years.

Fifteen houses were purchased during a few years' time, which made it possible to establish many new departments and classes. These houses were purchased at about six dollars a square foot of usable space, while new permanent construction would have cost approximately thirteen dollars a square foot. One of the houses was bought for $12,000 and a new Adult department was started. In four years' time those in the new department gave offerings totaling $36,000. Indeed, people do pay for themselves! It doesn't cost to provide space, it pays!

(2) *Make temporary use of garages, homes, and other buildings.*—A church in Maryland was started in a new housing area. It rented a small auditorium, but had no space for Sunday school departments and classes. Within an area of three or four blocks, members offered the use of their basements and other rooms of their homes for Sunday school. Six departments were thus located. They were so widely scattered that the Sunday school secretary had to use a motor scooter to get the records! But this temporary arrangement tided the church over until more adequate facilities could be found.

(3) *Build a new building.*—This of course is ideal. The new building can be planned to meet actual needs. It can challenge the people to give sacrificially to the worthy endeavor. It can make a strong testimony for Christ to the community. It can be one generation's contribution to the security of the rising generation.

Before attempting to build, be sure that the church house is well located with ample ground. Be sure that the planning and survey committee has made a thorough study of the needs before the building committee begins its work. By all means consult your state Sunday school secretary and the Church Architecture Department of the Baptist Sunday School Board for guidance. It will save you money, help to get what you want and need, and avoid many disappointing experiences.

III. BUILDING ADEQUATELY

In planning a new building it will be necessary to take a number of things into account.

1. *Consider the Space Requirements of the Various Age Groups*

You would not build all the rooms the same size, nor would you expect to provide for as many children as you would adults in a room of a given area. A Nursery child, for example, needs more space than an adult. The following table represents the average percentage of space needed for each age group in the Sunday school:

Nursery, 8 to 10 per cent
Beginner, 6 to 8 per cent
Primary, 8 to 10 per cent
Juniors, 10 to 12 per cent
Intermediates, 10 to 12 per cent
Young People, 12 to 16 per cent
Adults, 39 to 55 per cent

2. *Include Present and Potential Enrolment*

The percentage of space needed for each group varies in different communities because the age-group population varies. In new communities where there are many young families, the greatest need is provision for Nursery, Beginner, and perhaps Primary children, along with the young Adults and married Young People. The percentage of space needed by Juniors, Intermediates, and single Young People would probably be much lower than normal. In older communities and in downtown churches the percentage of Adults would be much larger than in other situations. In order to plan adequately, a church should make a careful study of the immediate community, the present enrolment, and the potential enrolment of the various age groups as revealed in a census.

3. Study Population Trends

A long-range program must take account of population trends. For the period 1959 to 1970, tremendous population increases are predicted for all age groups. The increase in some age groups will be much more pronounced than others. Based on the 1959 population, we can expect a percentage increase as follows:

Under four years, 17.5
Four to five years, 12.5
Six to eight years, 12.5
Nine to twelve years, 16.7
Thirteen to sixteen years, 39.9
Seventeen to twenty-four years, 56.9
Twenty-five to thirty-four years, 9.2
Thirty-five years and up, 11.4

Note that while there is a definite increase in all age groupings, Intermediates and Young People will show the greatest increases in comparison to the present number. The children of Beginner and older Cradle Roll or Nursery ages today will be Intermediates then.

4. Build Big Enough

It has been said that Baptists can fill anything they can build. Where there is the right spirit, a proper program, and good space, Baptist churches can continue reaching the people. The difficulty is in building big enough. Too often a church has planned a new building only to find that it was inadequate by the time they moved into it!

IV. SPACE AND EQUIPMENT NEEDS FOR EACH AGE GROUP

A building that is attractive and functional is another important factor in reaching people. The building will be used by all educational organizations and should, therefore, provide adequately for their needs.

All rooms should be easily accessible, and adequately ventilated, heated, and lighted. It is recommended that floors and cone bases be covered with linoleum, tile (asphalt, rubber, or vinyl), or hardwood.

Sunday schools and Training Unions no longer use classrooms below the Junior age group. Open rooms are best for Nursery, Beginner, and Primary children. At least one rest room should be provided for small children convenient to their department rooms.

It is recommended that all age groups except the Nursery have a piano.

Other essential space and equipment needs are listed by departmental age groups as follows:

CRADLE ROLL

1. A map of the area with the church territory districted
2. A selected room in the church for weekly meeting of workers
3. A storage closet or cabinet in the church for supplies
4. Space for an interest center in a conspicuous place
5. A table and bulletin board for the interest center
6. A Bible, Bible rack, and wall chart for the interest center

NURSERY

1. Rooms rectangular, with width to length as 4 is to 5
2. Floor space, 16 to 25 square feet (preferably 25) per enrolled person
3. Walls of light pastel colors
4. Windows of clear glass, the bottoms 24 inches from the floor
5. Supply cabinets on wall near the door, the bottoms 50 inches above the floor
6. Coat and hat rack for the workers
7. Movable coat and hat rack for two- and three-year-olds—may be placed under supply cabinet
8. Department Bible—1450BP

For Babies

1. Hospital cribs preferred (They are 27" by 42" and are of a safe depth.)
2. Bottle warmers in room or adjoining room

For Toddlers

1. Push-and-pull toys, large ball, interlocking train
2. Linen or plastic books
3. Doll, doll bed, and child's rocking chair
4. Blockbusters
5. Open shelves (10" by 30" and 27" high)
6. Rocking boat and steps combination, if space permits

For Two- or Three-Year-Olds

1. Table (24" by 36" and 20" high)
2. Chairs (10")
3. Plastic dishes
4. Doll, doll bed, and rocking chair
5. Bookrack and carefully selected books
6. Open shelves (10" by 30" and 27" high)
7. Record player and selected records
8. Wooden puzzles
9. Nature materials
10. Blocks

For additional information study **Improving Nursery Departments** by Polly Hargis Dillard.

BEGINNER

1. Open rooms, with 16 to 25 square feet per person (25 preferable—35 square feet needed if the room is used for weekday kindergarten)
2. Clear glass windows, not more than 20 inches from the floor
3. Supply cabinets attached to wall, bottoms 50" above floor
4. Picture rail 27 inches from the floor
5. Three shelf units (for blocks, nature materials, and art materials)
6. Department Bible—1450BP
7. Bookrack (33" high)
8. Table-cabinet for record player and recordings
9. Record player—No. VM 215
10. Cabinet-sink
11. Doll bed
12. Two tables (24" by 36" each)
13. One table for art activities (30" by 48")
14. Chairs: 10 inches high for 4's, and 12 inches high for 5's or for 4's and 5's together
15. Secretary's table
16. One adult chair
17. Coat racks for children and workers

For additional information and suggestions study the Beginner administration book and the sheet, "Beginner Department Equipment and Furnishings" published by the Beginner Committee and Church Architecture

Department, Baptist Sunday School Board, 127 Ninth Avenue, North, Nashville 3, Tennessee.

PRIMARY

1. Open room—16 to 25 square feet of floor space per person (preferably 25)
2. Coat rack for children and workers
3. Sunday school and Training Union picture file
4. Secretary's desk
5. Chair for secretary
6. Separate cabinet storage space for Sunday school, Training Union, and Sunbeam supplies
7. Art materials supply shelves
8. Work and study tables
9. Book rack
10. Nature shelves
11. Record player and table
12. Piano
13. Tackboard
14. Department Bible—1450BP
15. Chairs, 12 to 14 inches high
16. Have a separate department for every 30 boys and girls enrolled

JUNIOR

Department Assembly Room

1. An assembly room for each 4 to 8 classes, with 8 square feet of floor space per person
2. Superintendent's table
3. Secretary's table
4. Chairs 15 to 17 inches high (If floors are hardwood, use rubber tips on chairs.)
5. Supply cabinets or closets (one for Sunday School and one for Training Union)
6. Portable chalkboard
7. Provision for displays at front of assembly-matting, dado board, or picture rail
8. Portable metal rack for wraps
9. Department Bible—J910
10. Entrance to assembly at rear of room
11. Plastic-covered or wood folding doors between alternate classrooms for Training Union

Classrooms

1. Floor space 10 square feet per person
2. Chairs (15 to 17" high)
3. Work tables for creative activities
4. Chalkboard (portable wall board or built-in)
5. Ample tackboard (One wall may be covered with tackboard.)

INTERMEDIATE

Department Assembly Room

1. An assembly room for each 4 to 8 classes

2. Not less than 18 feet wide, and not more than twice the width in length
3. A minimum of 7 square feet of floor space per person
4. Entrance to assembly at rear of room
5. Ample wall space back of superintendent
6. Storage cabinet or closets for literature and supplies
7. Plastic-covered or wood folding doors between alternate classrooms for Training Union
8. Portable chalkboard
9. Comfortable chairs (16 to 18" high)
10. Superintendent's table and chair
11. Secretary's table and chair
12. Piano

Classrooms

1. A maximum of 9 pupils per classroom
2. Eight to ten square feet per person
3. A chalkboard and tackboard on side wall
4. Tablet armchair or small table for secretary
5. Comfortable chairs (16 to 18" high)
6. Container for supplies—table drawer, shelf, or cupboard
7. Hooks for wraps

YOUNG PEOPLE AND ADULT

Department Assembly Room

1. An assembly room for each 2 to 6 (8 absolute maximum) classes
2. Six to eight square feet of floor space per person
3. Assembly room located for easy accessibility (Married Young People and younger Adults should be convenient to the Nursery rooms. Avoid stairs for older Adults and, if possible, place them near the church auditorium.)
4. Entrance to assembly at rear of room
5. Ample wall space back of superintendent
6. Storage closets or cabinets for literature and supplies
7. Portable chalkboard
8. Tackboard located near exit of assembly room
9. Comfortable and movable chairs (18" high)
10. Department secretary's table
11. Piano
12. Superintendent's table and lectern if desired

Classrooms

1. As nearly square as possible for informal teaching
2. Classroom size to accommodate 12 to 20 persons—8 to 10 square feet of floor space per person
3. Portable chalkboard for each room
4. Tackboard on the wall of each room
5. Comfortable and movable chairs (preferably tablet-arm chairs, 18" high)
6. Teacher's table (no lectern or pulpit stand)

7. Tablet-arm chair or small table for secretary
8. Racks for hats and coats

EXTENSION

1. Room, preferably on main floor, for workers' meetings and supplies
2. Cabinet for supplies (with lock)
3. Chalkboard for reports
4. Space for interest-center table and bulletin board

V. Grow by Right Decisions

The future history of any church has already been accurately determined by the decisions it has made. Once a definite decision is reached, time is all that is required for the results of that decision to work out.

Some thirty years ago one of our thriving churches was a mission. Then it was organized into a church, and the time for a significant decision had come.

A small lot on which a small building could be constructed was available. Purchase of this lot had been proposed by some of the members. It was a lot the present group could easily pay for and one that would permit the erection of a small building to meet immediate needs. Another lot, larger and more expensive, also was available. It would give the church a better location and permit a greater ministry.

An earnest discussion developed in the church business meeting as to whether the church should locate and build for the present or, with greater vision and faith, build for the future. There were those who favored buying the small lot, erecting a small building that could readily be paid for, and being content with a small church doing a small work in a small way.

Others, however, felt that such a decision would be disastrous. A weak faith and a small program would limit what God could accomplish through that church. Finally, the minutes record, one of the members got up and poured out his heart in favor of a larger lot and bigger program. He concluded his appeal by waving his hat in the air and declaring: "If this church tonight will vote to purchase the larger property and build a larger building, out of my limited salary I will pledge $100.00 a month until every cent of the cost is paid."

The big men and women of that church—men and women of big heart, big faith, and big vision—prevailed, and the growth and increasing ministry of that church was assured. Through the years other such questions have been faced and right decisions have been made. The church today is what yesterday's decisions and the grace of God have made it.

As in this church, so in all churches. Decisions—right decisions—determine growth and ministry.

A church must continue to grow as long as there are unreached people.

When the present pattern of organization is saturated a larger pattern must be adopted.

The commission of Christ and the needs of the multitudes are the determining factors in the decisions a church must make.

WHAT WILL YOU DO?

Based on your study of this chapter, write down your honest conviction about the decisions your church needs to make in regard to providing space and equipment.

CHAPTER 6

I. GOALS AND GETTING THE JOB DONE
 1. The Goal Must Be Worthy
 2. The Problems Must Be Understood
 3. The Program Must Be Big
 4. Togetherness Must Mark the Effort

II. GOALS FOR THE YEAR AHEAD
 1. Use Preparation Week for Goal Setting and Planning
 2. Set Goals Wisely
 3. Consider a Goal Sheet

III. GOALS AS A PROGRAM OF WORK
 1. Standards Give Stability and Balance
 2. Standards Guide Co-operative Action
 3. Standards Must Be Used Wisely

IV. ACHIEVING GOALS THROUGH USING RECORDS
 1. Get Good Records
 2. Let Records Help Get Better Work Done
 3. Magnify Records for Individual Spiritual Growth

V. GOALS AND THE IMAGE OF THE FUTURE

A Church Using Goals for Developing Sunday School Work

A MAN watched for some time as a young boy whittled on a piece of wood. "What are you making, son?" he asked.

"Well, sir, I ain't exactly thought about that."

"But you must be making something," insisted the man.

After a moment, the youngster replied, "Oh, yes, sir, it'll come out to be something or other. It always does."

Our Sunday schools always turn out to be something or other, but do they turn out to be what God intends them to be or what the churches want them to be?

I. GOALS AND GETTING THE JOB DONE

Goals are important to progress. They help us get somewhere. They help us accomplish what ought to be done.

1. *The Goal Must Be Worthy*

Jesus recognized the necessity for the ultimate goal if an individual is to be constantly challenged. "Be ye perfect," is an impossible objective, but nothing short of such a standard in the realm of the spiritual will be adequate to draw out from a man his best.

Said Paul, "I press toward the mark for the prize of the high calling of God in Christ Jesus" (Phil. 3:14). In these words he expressed a profound and basic law. A person develops along the lines of the standards and ideals that he has accepted for himself. What one genuinely aspires to become deeply affects his life.

91

As it is with a Christian, so must it be with a church. The lack of challenge often is at the root of failure to move out in service for God. God's expectancy is great. His assignment is to the ends of the earth. He waits for a church to respond to his challenge.

2. The Problems Must Be Understood

This is not negative thinking. There are difficulties to be overcome. Often they are magnified out of all proportion. However, in order to achieve the purpose of the Sunday school program for your church, it will be necessary to know who or what stands in the way of success. Is it lack of a strong motive? Is it insufficient workers? It is untrained workers? Is it absence of a strong visitation program? Is it failure to plan a practical program that will produce results?

Not the problems, but the needs must become the dominating factor. The need of lost souls for the message of hope! The need of homes for Christian parents! The need of the Sunday school teacher for adequate help! The need of the little child for the guidance of a loving, sympathetic teacher. Let the needs determine the plans, and the plans will be big enough to override the problems.

3. The Program Must Be Big

"Expect great things of God, attempt great things for God." Nothing short of such a spirit will be equal to the opportunities God has granted to our churches. It is up to the leaders of a church to offer a big program.

One church had stood in a lovely rural area for seventy-five years. The members were God-fearing, generous, and kind—good salt-of-the-earth people. Yet, somehow there was lack of vision, lack of challenge, and lack of a program. For years the Sunday school had not gone beyond five classes, with an enrolment of one hundred. Then the pastor and the Sunday school superintendent became aroused. They called the people together and studied the possibilities of an enlarged program. Soon in the one-room building, there were twelve classes (separated by curtains) and two hundred people were enrolled. Before long there was a new brick church house and a fully departmentized Sunday school, with thirty classes and four hundred enrolled.

Tower Grove Baptist Church in St. Louis, Missouri, located in a vast Catholic population, has achieved unusual growth in every phase of its work in recent years. From 1956 to 1959 Sunday school enrolment grew from 2,059 to 3,500; average attendance moved from 1,100 to 1,700; baptisms increased from 29 to 115; church income grew from $210,709 to $310,000. How did all of this come about? Goals were set and achieved in the areas of finding the people, expanding the organization, enlarging the building, training the workers, and going after the prospects!

4. Togetherness Must Mark the Effort

Leaders must take the lead. They must think big and propose a big program.

One church follows the practice of calling the Sunday school cabinet together each fall to work out specific goals for the year. For example, in 1957 and 1958 the following goals were agreed upon, with the indicated results:

	1957		1958	
	Goal	Attainment	Goal	Attainment
Sunday School Enrolment	3,200	3,215	3,500	3,508
Average Attendance	1,500	1,398	1,650	1,570
Baptisms	150	162	175	261

Setting the goals was a joint project, and the achievement of the goals was the joint concern and effort of the fifty-one departments in the school, each department setting its own goal as a pro rata share of the total.

Success depends upon group togetherness in setting and achieving goals. At the outset of the new Sunday school year, every worker should have a clear conception of what the school as a whole and what he individually is attempting to accomplish.

The same spiritual objectives hold every year, but workers need constant reindoctrination! Newly recruited workers need a spiritual interpretation of their task. Specific objectives need to be set out, interpreted, and adopted by all the workers at the year's beginning.

II. GOALS FOR THE YEAR AHEAD

Southern Baptist gains in Sunday school work have been in proportion to deliberate and specific goals. We have learned that by working together and giving united emphasis to great major objectives year by year, we make progress.

1. *Use Preparation Week for Goal Setting and Planning*

Preparation Week is a priority activity for any church. The value of this week is becoming more apparent every year. Where progress is expected, planning is imperative.

A recent survey was made in one of our states that showed an unusually fine gain in Sunday school enrolment, twice the average for the entire Convention. It was discovered that a large proportion of the churches had observed Preparation Week the year before and set the stage for progress in their Sunday school program.

(1) *Preparation Week prepares for growth.*—Many worthy purposes may be achieved through Preparation Week, but essentially it is a time for setting goals, expanding organization, installing new officers, occupying new space, and in general getting ready for growth.

(2) *Prepare for Preparation Week.*—The last week in September is not the time to begin to set goals and make plans. Actually, it is a time for launching previously conceived plans. Preparation for a proper observance of Preparation Week should begin in June, July, and August.

The suggested date for Preparation Week each year is the full week in September which immediately precedes Promotion Day. This timing is deliberate, because specific plans for establishing new units, rearranging space, and other essential changes should be launched with the beginning of the new Sunday school year, October 1.

It would be helpful to appoint a number of study committees as you prepare for Preparation Week:

—A study group to consider the calendar of activities for the Sunday school, which you plan to present for consideration and adoption during Preparation Week

—A study group to recommend goals for the year

—A study group to consider needs for an expanded organization and additional space

—A study group to work out the program and schedule for Preparation Week, build attendance, and work to make the week successful

Each year a *Sunday School Planning Booklet* is mailed out in June to pastors, superintendents, and ministers of education. This booklet gives detailed help in planning for Preparation Week. The September issue of *The Sunday School Builder* contains added resource materials for making the week effective.

(3) *Preparation assures the best year next year.*—Someone has said that a good preacher is always going to preach his best sermon next time, a good Sunday school teacher is going to teach the best lesson next Sunday. Certainly, every good Sunday school superintendent is planning for the next year to be the best for his Sunday school.

Something new can be added when you observe Preparation Week: a new class, a new department, a new Sunday school, a new emphasis on evangelism, a new start in visitation. Failure to start something new will inevitably result in failure to grow.

Plan big enough through Preparation Week. It is all too

easy to let good work stand in the way of the best; to set good aims, but not good enough; to make big plans, but not big enough. The churches that have shown great growth and have produced great fruit in souls redeemed and lives transformed have been those churches that have planned and prepared to attempt great things for the Lord.

Plan big, and next year your church can reach, teach, and win to Christ many lost souls.

The reason for all of the work of a New Testament church is that somebody is lost. And that *somebody* has grown to the tragic number of more than forty million lost people living within the bounds of our Southern Baptist territory. You have them in your community; you will find them in your present Sunday school enrolment; you will find them in the families of your church membership.

Great days are upon our churches—days of opportunity, days of responsibility, days of privilege. We must not be shortsighted when men of vision are so sorely needed. We must not be lukewarm when hearts on fire will turn the tide of the battle. We must not be backward when God would have us stand forth to make a mighty conquest in his name.

2. *Set Goals Wisely*

Each church, of course, will determine its own goals. Some special emphases are offered year by year in the planning booklet mailed to all of the churches. But each year goals should be set in three broad areas:

(1) *Set goals in enlargement*—Somehow we must increase the number of people being reached for Bible study. If a Sunday school is not growing, then no amount of emphasis on improvement can make up for that lack.

Preparation Week sets the direction and the pace; it largely determines the amount of growth. What will your school determine to do regarding increased enrolment for next year? Consider the increase suggested by the following chart. Prayerfully consider what it means in terms of your Sunday school.

SUGGESTED GOALS FOR ENROLMENT GAINS

Where Present Enrolment Is	Set a Goal for Gain of
Under 100	40% or more
100–299	30% or more
300–499	20% or more
500–999	15% or more
1,000–1,999	10% or more
2,000–up	5% or more

When you have determined worthy enrolment gains, then you will include some definite goals for the accomplishment of the increase in the enrolment, including new units, new space, additional workers, new Sunday schools, more visitation.

(2) *Set goals for improvement.*—Every year goals should be set for improvement in the kind and quality of work: better workers, better teaching, better living. Ways and means of accomplishing such improvement would be spelled out in the goals: doing a better job of enlisting officers and teachers, lifting the standards of the workers, offering a training program for the development of better teaching, inspiring pupils to live the truths they profess.

(3) *Set goals for evangelism.*—Will you not think in terms of the goal of making the Sunday school positively evangelistic, of seeking to develop every Sunday school worker into a personal soul-winner, and of planning specific ways in which Sunday school workers may be trained in how to win the lost to Christ?

3. *Consider a Goal Sheet*

The goal sheet pictured contains a check list of possible goals for your Sunday school. It may be revised and adapted to your specific needs at any time.

A SAMPLE GOAL SHEET

This year we shall seek to achieve the following goals. (Check to the left and enter figures where needed.)

_____Take a religious census second Sunday in September.

_____Observe Harvest Day third Sunday in September.

_____Observe Preparation Week (full week in September preceding Promotion Day).

_____Observe January Bible Study Week.

_____Participate in church revival meetings.

_____Observe Christian Home Week in May.

_____Participate in associational group or central training schools.

_____Conduct a Vacation Bible school in our church.

_____Promote a weekly visitation program.

_____Use effectively the Six Point Record System.

_____Conduct a weekly officers and teachers' meeting.

_____Promote parent-worker meetings.

_____Plan to start _____ new departments and classes.

_____Work for a net enrolment gain of _____ or _____ per cent.

_____Work for an increase in attendance of _____ per cent.

_____Number of baptisms _____

_____Number of Standard units _____ (school, department, classes, and groups)

_____Number of awards in Church Study Course for Teaching and Training _____. Awards in category 17 _____

_____Provide Bible Survey Plan.

_____Number of new branch Sunday schools or missions _____

_____Number of mission Vacation Bible schools _____

III. Goals as a Program of Work

The Standards of Excellence are both goals and programs for good Sunday school administration. They have been developed out of the crucible of experience as leaders have sought to follow the Holy Spirit's guidance and to conform to the principles and doctrines taught in the Word of God. The blueprint for building a good Sunday school is found in the Standards.

Here is a Sunday school that had shown a loss of 150 in Sunday school enrolment in the face of gains in nearby churches. The church adopted the Standards for the Sunday school and the various units. The pastor used the principles in the Standards as a basis for sermons in the Sunday morning preaching services for several weeks. The church came to understand that the Standards provide a basic program which enables the church to win more people to Christ. In less than one year a net enrolment increase of 125 was reported with 23 Standard units in the Sunday school, and nearly 400 training awards.

1. *Standards Give Stability and Balance*

Sunday schools must be anchored to right objectives and committed to right methods. It is easy to lose clarity of purpose and definiteness of objective unless some basic working goals have been established. Standards embody fundamental principles. In the words of J. N. Barnette:

> The Standard magnifies the church, anchors the Sunday school to the church, and trains Sunday school members to be good church members. We make no apologies for our Standards. They have anchored our work to the Bible, the church, and the people. They have given us right directions. . . . They have unified our work.

Churches everywhere testify that achieving the Standard has lifted the level of their Sunday school work, has strengthened weak areas, and has created a better spirit of co-operation among the workers. We are taught in the Bible to "prove all things; hold fast that which is good" (1 Thess. 5:21). For half a century Southern Baptist churches have proved the principles which are written into the Standards.

2. Standards Guide Co-operative Action

As Sunday schools grow in size and expand in organization, there is increasing necessity for a means of securing unity of purpose and co-operative action. Such means has been provided in the Standards for all units. The same essential principles are apparent in all the Standards.

3. Standards Must Be Used Wisely

The Sunday school Standards have been developed to make quite objective the essential functions of a Sunday school, a department, a class, or a group. They have been derived from the best experience of numberless churches. Drawn out of specific situations, they have universal application. They can benefit your school. Consider these points in the wise use of Standards:

(1) *Standards are not all-inclusive.*—They do not include all the things a Sunday school should do, but they are sound and good. They have been tested by experience. They deserve consideration and use. They will help to avoid costly mistakes. They will point out weaknesses. They will help to keep the work of your school on its course!

(2) *The Standards set out minimum, not maximum, performance.*—Where percentages are used, they are not to limit but to help lift the work at least to this minimum level. Standards must never set a ceiling on performance. They are not set to supply satisfaction, but to encourage effort.

(3) *Standards are for guidance, not motivation.*—Perhaps the greatest enemy to the Standards and to our work has been the unwitting use of the urge to "reach the Standard."

Our work needs a stronger motive than that. "The love of Christ constraineth us" (2 Cor. 5:14).

(4) *Standards have value even when not fully attained.*— The widespread influence of the Standards cannot be measured by the numbers of units that have attained recognition. The influence of the Standards is seen in the principles that have become fixed in the thinking of our workers, in the directions that have been established, and in the acceleration of worthy achievements that have come about through the use of Standards.

IV. Achieving Goals Through Using Records

Any business organization that makes progress not only sets goals, but keeps accurate records. The Sunday school is engaged in the greatest business in the world. True, it is spiritual business, operated by spiritual power, but our Master encourages us to learn from "the children of this world" (Luke 16:8).

1. *Get Good Records*

The basic information needed by workers and pupils can be provided through the use of the Six Point Record System. It has forms adapted to every size Sunday school. (See *The Six Point Record System and Its Use* by Emma Noland.)

How do records relate to the achievement of goals?

(1) *A classification plan makes it possible to know the people who are enrolled.*—Classification Slip, Form 10, should be filled out completely for every new member and visitor. The slip may be filled out by the general secretary or by classification officers placed in the departments or at other convenient places.

(2) *Permanent enrolment records help to keep individuals on roll.*—When a new member has been enrolled and assigned to the proper department and class, the general secretary should make up a permanent Enrolment Card, Form 20,

and place in the alphabetical file. This is the official Sunday school roll, and no name should be removed except by approval of the general superintendent. The enrolment card remains in the master file and is brought up to date each year as the pupil is promoted. Duplicate file cards may be made for the department enrolment file.

(3) *The Individual Report Envelope is at the heart of the record system.*—It should be filled out individually by every member, Junior age and above, in attendance each Sunday. The workers will make the records for Nursery, Beginner, and Primary children. Nursery children are graded on attendance only; Primary and Beginner children, on attendance and on time. The workers and all pupils Junior age and above are graded on six points. Under the proper supervision of the teachers and workers, individual records can be secured efficiently and with spiritual emphasis.

(4) *Summary reports reveal strong and weak points.*—Individual reports should be secured early in the Sunday school session. Class reports should be totaled on the Class Record Card, Form 35Q, checked by the teacher or the class secretary and sent to the department secretary, who totals the report for the department and sends it to the general secretary. (See leaflets on Nursery, Beginner, and Primary work for instructions about the records for these age groups.) In nondepartment schools the general secretary would make the record by classes.

The Cradle Roll, Extension, and Young People Away departments make their reports monthly.

(5) *The teacher's record book aids in pupil-study.*—The appropriate record book, kept up to date, will furnish invaluable information for any teacher who seriously seeks to minister to the individual needs of his members. This record contains, in addition to the weekly six point record, information about the pupil's date of birth, address, family, church membership, school or place of business, and other items.

(6) *Monthly reports help to relate the school to church.*—Since the Sunday school is an agency of the church, it should give a regular accounting of its ministry, thus keeping the church informed and interested in the work of the Sunday school.

2. Let Records Help Get Better Work Done

Records, like any other tool, may be wisely or unwisely used. Consider some positive suggestions for their use.

(1) *Use records in the right spirit.*—While high individual and class grades are desirable, magnifying grades can easily take the attention off the spiritual values. By all means, grade consciousness should be avoided.

Classes should not seek to manipulate records in order to maintain high grades. When love motivates, there will be no reluctance to enrol the person who may "pull down the class grade." Remember, we are in the business of enrolling people. Let us not make it hard for any individual to get on the roll. Of course, workers will verify the enrolment and the classification information for each child.

Once an individual is enrolled, it is the responsibility of the Sunday school to maintain his interest and hold him for attendance. Let us make it easy for a person to enrol in the Sunday school, but very hard to get off the roll.

(2) *Make the records promote attendance.*—Records may be used effectively in the promotion of visitation and in maintaining good attendance. From time to time, display the enrolment and attendance records of classes and departments. Graphs of various types are effective visual aids in studying comparative enrolment and attendance.

(3) *Use the records to evaluate accomplishments.*—Records are instruments for evaluating the work done by classes, departments, and individuals. Some superintendents always have a growing department; others show losses. Effective teaching is revealed by preaching attendance and support

of the church financial program on the part of class members.

(4) *Records provide information for additional planning.* —When a thorough analysis of last Sunday's records is presented at the weekly officers and teachers' meeting on Wednesday night, each worker's task is laid out for him for the week! One of the most vital parts of the workers' meeting should be this careful study of records in order to locate definitely the weak points or omissions of each member of the Sunday school.

The attendance records of some of the larger Adult classes indicate a need for new classes. The record of one such class with 108 members appeared as follows when divided into five-year age spans for sake of analysis.

Age Groups	No. Enrolled	Per Cent Attending
25–29	8	15
30–34	23	41
35–39	27	45
40–44	29	47
45–49	15	21
50–54	6	16

It is obvious that the 35–39 and the 40–44 age groups form the core of the class and that the other groupings are not at all compatible. If classes could be provided for each of the five-year groupings, undoubtedly the attendance would be about the same in all groups.

(5) *Records furnish incentive and guidance for evangelism.*—Lost people who are enrolled in Sunday school and who attend with some regularity provide the most immediate evangelistic opportunities. Records of unsaved prospects call for renewed effort to enrol them in Sunday school in order to provide a better evangelistic opportunity. Experience shows that each year approximately one out of every three lost people enrolled in our Sunday schools is won to Christ, while only about one out of every 240 not enrolled is won.

3. *Magnify Records for Individual Spiritual Growth*

Properly used, the Six Point Record System becomes a pupil program for spiritual growth. If pupils are to grow spiritually, should they not associate themselves with Christian people who are trying to find and follow God's will? Should they not follow a planned course of Bible study? Would you not urge that they practice stewardship of possessions? Certainly to hear the Word preached and to share in the worship services is an indispensable element in spiritual growth. The activities listed are fundamentally the content of the Six Point Record System.

V. Goals and the Image of the Future

The goals of an institution or a person are his image of the future. Goals are faith given expression, and "faith is the substance of things hoped for" (Heb. 11:1).

Fred Polak, in *The Future Is Past Tense,* has pointed out that if a people, a nation, a community, or a group has positive and optimistic ideas, and a dynamic aspiration, it will grow and prosper. If, on the other hand, it shows a hesitant attitude and an uncertain purpose, it is in for serious trouble and almost certain disintegration. By developing a clear image of what is desired in the future and by careful planning, man creates that same future according to the image developed in his mind.

A church also grows toward its ideals and objectives. What are the ideals of your church? What are its "images of the future"? Do they center on four fundamentals: people, the Bible, Jesus, and discipleship?

WHAT WILL YOU DO?

There seems only one thing to do after studying this chapter: Working together as a group, determine the goals your church should set and reach this year.

CHAPTER 7

I. TEACHING THE WORD—THE CHARACTERISTIC MINISTRY OF THE SUNDAY SCHOOL
   1. Bible Teaching Must Magnify the Churches
   2. Bible Teaching Must Satisfy Human Need
   3. The Sunday School Is Equipped to Teach

II. MEETING SPIRITUAL NEEDS—THE CHIEF AIM OF BIBLE TEACHING
   1. Objectives Are Based on the Bible and Human Need
   2. Objectives for Christian Teaching and Training Have Been Formulated
   3. Objectives Are Adapted to Each Age Group
   4. Objectives Must Be Effectively Used

III. BIBLE STUDY—THE PROGRAM OF THE SUNDAY SCHOOL
   1. The Entire Sunday Morning Session Is for Teaching
   2. The Vacation Bible School Extends the Sunday School
   3. The Weekday Bible Study Program Complements the Sunday School
   4. The Sunday School Joins Hands with the Home

IV. BETTER TEACHING—THE PURPOSE OF THE WEEKLY OFFICERS AND TEACHERS' MEETING
   1. The Values Are Significant
   2. Teaching Improvement Is Magnified
   3. The Best Lesson Materials Should Be Provided and Used

V. OTHER OPPORTUNITIES FOR IMPROVEMENT OF TEACHING
   1. Make Full Use of the Church Study Course for Teaching and Training
   2. Magnify the Bible Survey Plan
   3. Promote Preview Studies
   4. Use January Bible Study Week
   5. Encourage Proper Use of Visual Aids
   6. Capitalize on Every Opportunity for Improvement

VI. THE TEACHER OF TEACHERS

7

A Church Getting Better Bible Teaching Done

SUNDAY SCHOOLS are not failures. They are touching the lives of forty-two million children, youth, and adults in our land. Sunday schools are quickening spiritual interests, pointing men and women and boys and girls to the Saviour, and providing scriptural truth on which lives can be safely built. More than seven million people are enrolled in Southern Baptist Sunday schools. Our stewardship is great because our entrustment is great, our opportunity is great, and our obligation is inescapable.

Sunday schools are not failing, neither are they doing all they can do and must do to make God's Word known and loved and lived. Because of all that is at stake we must reach more and teach better. Something of what is involved in our glorious task of teaching has been caught up by W. L. Howse in his book *Those Treasured Hours:*

The Bible is not an ordinary book, and no class session is an ordinary period of time. When the teacher reads the Bible, God speaks. This Book is a lamp and a light. People in sin are in spiritual darkness. The Bible tells of Jesus, the Light of the world, the Saviour of mankind. The entire Bible points to Christ, the Lord and Master of life. When one takes this library of sixty-six books into his classroom and teaches from it, he is dealing with the most unusual Book in the world, the most unusual message in the world, and is spending the most important time in the world.[1]

[1] Howse, *Those Treasured Hours*, (Nashville: Broadman Press, 1960), pp. 5–6.

I. Teaching the Word—The Characteristic Ministry of the Sunday School

It is a truism that Bible teaching is the distinctive function of the Sunday school. What are some significant principles involved in that function?

1. *Bible Teaching Must Magnify the Churches*

In the Bible, Baptists find their message and mission. The Bible magnifies the church as the divinely ordained institution through which the message is to be proclaimed. Bible teaching must impress minds and hearts with the responsibility which Christ has placed upon his churches. God has promised, "My word . . . shall not return unto me void" (Isa. 55:11). But God has chosen to guarantee and stabilize his program through teaching churches.

2. *Bible Teaching Must Satisfy Human Need*

Every great spiritual awakening in the world's history has been preceded by widespread, intensive Bible study. We claim, without apology, that the enlistment of the unreached multitudes and their enrolment in effective Bible study is the paramount need of our day.

Bible study is needed to counteract the disillusionment occasioned by the failure of science to solve human problems. Because of the wonderful advances made by science, people have looked upon material resources for the satisfaction of man's need. Now, when science is at its zenith in achievement, man's predicament is the most pronounced and hopeless. The remedy will come through the cultivation of the knowledge of truth as it is in God's Word.

Bible study is needed to restore a correct conception of God. Nature reveals God as Creator; science may reveal God as Lawgiver; but the Bible alone reveals God as Father and Saviour.

Bible study is needed to reveal a wholesome concept of man. Where God is not known men are not valued. What the Bible teaches about the worth of man in the eyes of God will establish his value in the eyes of men. Make no mistake about it, nothing short of Christianity will guarantee the security of the individual either in time or eternity.

Other ideologies appeal to the desire for economic or political security, but even these secondary securities cannot be permanently had apart from the knowledge that man is created in the image of God and ransomed by the atoning blood of Jesus.

3. *The Sunday School Is Equipped to Teach*

Even a casual review reminds us how remarkably is the Sunday school designed and arranged to teach.

The textbook is God's Word, the Book of Life.

The place is the church building, God's house with the sanction and atmosphere of his spirit.

The time is Sunday, the Lord's Day in a special sense.

The curriculum materials, the Bible study helps, the resources are carefully planned and provided according to the need, interest, and ability level of the pupils.

The situation for effective learning comes about in well-arranged, well-equipped rooms, with small graded groups of pupils, and through methods suited to the way pupils learn best.

The teachers and workers are volunteers who, with love and dedication, are able to grow in effectiveness of technique even as they already possess the essential element of heart power.

The promise of the Father is unto those who seek to carry

out his commission: "And, lo, I am with you alway, even unto the end of the world."

II. Meeting Spiritual Needs—The Chief Aim of Bible Teaching

Christian teaching is the only kind of education that involves the whole personality and particularly the spiritual element of personality, which colors and determines the other aspects. A clear statement of aims or objectives in teaching is vital, for what is taught and how we teach it necessarily reflect the beliefs we hold and our assumptions about life and what it is for.

1. *Objectives Are Based on the Bible and Human Need*

Revealed truth is the basis of our teaching. This fact makes a vast difference in our objectives and in our philosophy of education itself. Objectives for the Christian teacher are clearly set out in the Bible.

One such statement is found in Ephesians 4:13. Phillips translates it: "That the whole body might be built up until the time comes when, in the unity of common faith and common knowledge of the Son of God, we arrive at real maturity." [2]

The inspired Word is useful for "teaching the faith and correcting error, for resetting the direction of a man's life and training him in good living" [3] (2 Tim. 3:16–17 Phillips translation).

Bible-centered objectives are concerned with persons. Therefore, the basic spiritual needs of individuals must be considered when specific objectives for Christian teaching and training are stated.

[2] J. B. Phillips, *The New Testament in Modern English* (New York: The Macmillan Co., 1958).
[3] *Ibid.*

2. Objectives for Christian Teaching and Training Have Been Formulated

After several years of intensive and extensive study by the Curriculum Committee of the Baptist Sunday School Board, a statement of objectives has been developed which is Bible-centered and related to the needs of people at each age level.

OBJECTIVES

of Christian Teaching and Training

The overarching objective is to help persons become aware of God as revealed in Jesus Christ, respond to him in a personal commitment of faith, strive to follow him in the full meaning of Christian discipleship, live in conscious recognition of the guidance and power of the Holy Spirit, and grow toward the goal of Christian maturity.

1. **Christian conversion.**—Our aim is to lead each person to a genuine experience of the forgiving and saving grace of God through Jesus Christ.

2. **Church membership.**—Our aim is to guide each Christian into intelligent, active, and devoted membership in a New Testament church.

3. **Christian worship.**—Our aim is to help each person to make Christian worship a vital and constant part of his expanding experience.

4. **Christian knowledge and conviction.**—Our aim is to help each person to grow toward mature Christian knowledge, understanding, and conviction.

5. **Christian attitudes and appreciation.**—Our aim is to assist each person in developing such Christian attitudes and appreciations that he will have a Christian approach to all of life.

6. **Christian living.**—Our aim is to guide each person in developing habits and skills which promote spiritual growth and in applying Christian standards of conduct in every area of life.

7. **Christian service.**—Our aim is to lead each person to invest his talents and skills in Christian service.[4]

---

3. Objectives Are Adapted to Each Age Group

In each of the seven areas, objectives of Christian teaching and training have been adapted to the essential needs and

[4] Prepared by the Curriculum Committee of the Sunday School Board of the Southern Baptist Convention, Nashville, Tennessee. © 1960.

ability level of the respective age groups. These age-group aims form the basis for organizing and planning curriculum materials for each of the church organizations and for guiding the workers in what they seek to accomplish. For a complete statement of these objectives, refer to *The Curriculum Guide* (Convention Press, 1960).

4. Objectives Must Be Effectively Used

How are these objectives used and how do they become truly effective?

(1) *They must be clear and definite for the teacher or worker.*—When teaching or any other educative activity lacks purpose, it has little meaning. Every worker needs to know specifically what he is attempting to accomplish in the lives of his pupils. These objectives must be worthy and challenging, must be in keeping with the need and ability of the pupils, and must be stated in terms of what pupils can and should do about them. Every member of the class or department needs to be included in these purposes. Every lesson or activity or program should be seen as an opportunity to take a forward step in achieving the ultimate purposes for each individual. Such clarity of purpose on the part of every worker will sharpen preparation and put meaning into the experience for teachers and pupils alike.

(2) *Objectives must be shared by all workers.*—Bringing Christian truth to bear on a personality is a lifetime process. It cannot all be accomplished at any one period or through any one approach. There are needs at each stage which must be met at that time and which have a bearing on the needs at each succeeding stage of life. We are concerned with the individual who is progressing through various stages of life and levels of need. As workers we need to know him as a whole person. It will help us to know what has been at-

tempted for him and with him in the age group which precedes our contact, and what will be attempted in the age group following our contribution. Conceived of in this way, the Sunday school and other organizations in the church can truly be an organized responsibility for providing essential guidance to the spiritual growth and development of the pupils.

(3) *Objectives must be accepted by the learners.*—The aims of the teachers must become the learning goals of the pupils or little will be accomplished. If the objectives have been taken from the Bible and if they also grow out of the basic needs of the individual, this will not be too difficult. The secret of success in teaching is to help pupils to recognize their needs and to motivate and guide the pupils in satisfying those needs.

III. Bible Study—The Program of the Sunday School

The varied phases of the Sunday school program need to be properly understood in their relationship to Bible study.

1. *The Entire Sunday Morning Session Is for Teaching*

Not thirty minutes but seventy-five minutes and more are devoted to Bible teaching on Sunday morning in a well-ordered Sunday school. Sunday school begins for the child as soon as he arrives. For the little children there is activity time and (beginning with the older Nursery ages) group time. In the Junior age there is early time, class time, and the department assembly. For ages above the Junior the order is reversed. Alert teachers and class officers seek to utilize wisely the informal teaching opportunities before the assembly begins.

The whole Sunday school period is one program, devoted to Bible teaching, and leading into a meaningful worship experience in the preaching service.

2. *The Vacation Bible School Extends the Sunday School*

The Vacation Bible school ministry has extended a concentrated and effective Bible study opportunity for boys
and girls into the vacation time. A two-weeks' school offers
thirty additional hours of Bible study.

The Sunday school superintendent is responsible for the
Vacation Bible school, as he is for any other phase of Sunday school work. Under his supervision and direction the
faculty will be secured, the time for the school set, and necessary preparations made. The curriculum materials for the
Vacation Bible school have been prepared and presented in
such a way as to supplement the courses of Bible study offered in the Sunday school and to include additional related
activities that make Vacation Bible school truly an attractive
and profitable experience for the boys and girls.

Since Vacation Bible school work came to be a definite
phase of the Sunday school program, tremendous gains have
been realized until now the enrolment in Vacation Bible
school is approximately 40 per cent as great as the Sunday
school enrolment.

3. *The Weekday Bible Study Program Complements the Sunday School*

A growing development in providing additional Bible
study opportunities through the Sunday school comes in the
weekday Bible study program. It is designed for children and
youth of ages nine through seventeen (or through high
school). It is a church-centered program of Christian education designed to complement what is being done through
Sunday school, Training Union, Vacation Bible school, and
other educational approaches for children of the ages involved.

The Bible study provided in the weekday program is distinctive in approach and in method. A specialized curriculum

calls for a textbook study of the Bible with assignments and activities on the academic level of courses offered by public schools. Since Bible study cannot be offered in our public schools, a one-hour session each week provided by our churches can meet a need for this type of Bible study in thousands of our churches.

Curriculum materials for this study will probably be available by 1962, for the churches desiring to use them.

Another aspect of the weekday program that has Bible teaching possibilities is the church kindergarten. The kindergarten is a ministry of the church to five-year-olds throughout the week. It enables the church to make greater use of buildings dedicated to Christian education. It provides a Christian environment in which children can grow and develop in a wholesome manner. It aids in reaching and ministering to unchurched families.

Further information may be had by writing to the Sunday School Department of the Baptist Sunday School Board, Nashville 3, Tennessee.

4. *The Sunday School Joins Hands with the Home*

The Sunday school must bear a heavy responsibility of working with the parents in Christian teaching. Other organizations of the church also work with the homes. However, the Sunday school has a distinctive responsibility to a large number of parents who have not yet been reached by other agencies.

Sunday school workers visit in the homes, encourage parents to make effective use of the literature provided them, urge parents to participate in the study of the age-group books in the Church Study Course for Teaching and Training, and provide regular parent-teacher meetings. Through these and other means the Sunday school seeks to accomplish the ideal of parents and teachers working together in Christian teaching.

IV. BETTER TEACHING—THE PURPOSE OF THE WEEKLY OF-
FICERS AND TEACHERS' MEETING

The nerve center for the entire Sunday school is the weekly
officers and teachers' meeting. Without it there is poor communication, lack of direction, inadequate preparation, and a
host of other handicaps to the work.

1. *The Values Are Significant*

Clearly, the advantages of holding regular weekly officers
and teachers' meetings outweigh any objections. Of course it
takes time to have the meeting, but no more time than it
takes to get ready for the responsibilities in any other way. It
takes time to plan the work and to prepare for assembly programs and class sessions.

(1) *The weekly officers and teachers' meeting provides
a gentle discipline for individual preparation.*—The routine
is an incentive to the workers for planning and preparation.
Every officer and teacher must make reports and indicate
plans for Sunday. Without regular meetings these things
could easily slip by without attention.

(2) *It provides good fellowship.*—Working together as
an effective team develops understanding, good personal relationships, and warm spirit among the officers and teachers.

(3) *It makes possible purposeful prayer.*—Every week
there is need and occasion for such prayer—for the indifferent members, the prospects, the lost pupils, and for the
guidance of the Holy Spirit in program and lesson preparation. Purposeful prayer binds workers together.

(4) *It makes finding potential workers much easier.*—A
Sunday school which conducts effective weekly officers and
teachers' meetings can, by the quality of work produced and
the spirit developed, make the enlistment of additional
workers easier than it would otherwise be.

(5) *It provides on-the-job training for the leaders.*—In the

weekly meeting each participant has opportunity to grow spiritually, to learn more of the needs of his pupils, and to understand more clearly how spiritual needs of the pupils may be met.

(6) *It encourages closer co-operation.*—Before there can be wholehearted co-operation between workers there must be mutual acceptance of common objectives. The weekly meeting helps to keep the working goals of the Sunday school and of all the departments centered in these major emphases: Discover all who should be reached; visit all who are discovered; enrol all who are visited; teach all who are enrolled; win all who are taught; enlist all who are won.

(7) *It gives attention to the conditions conducive to good teaching.*—A regular meeting of the workers provides the opportunity to make adjustments as needed in the time schedule, to improve the arrangement and usage of space and equipment, to supervise the size of the classes, to plan for more effective assembly programs, to develop skill in securing the participation of pupils, and to study the records in order to discover possible places where the program is not as effective as it should be.

2. *Teaching Improvement Is Magnified*

The weekly workers' meeting has as its primary purpose a continuous training and development of the leaders in the Sunday school so that they will be more able to share with their pupils.

Of major concern is consideration of the principles of effective teaching and especially how these principles may be applied to particular lessons. Many workers have discovered that one of the most useful features of the weekly meeting is to share in the planning for next Sunday's lesson. Each worker makes preparation for next Sunday's teaching according to a plan sheet. Then in group discussion each one shares in the benefit of the preparation of the others.

Specific guidance for these meetings can be found in free leaflets on the weekly officers and teachers' meeting, from the study course book *Building Better Sunday Schools Through the Weekly Officers and Teachers' Meeting* by G. S. Dobbins, and by use of the suggested program materials carried in *The Sunday School Builder*.

3. *The Best Lesson Materials Should Be Provided and Used*

Every teacher and pupil should receive the lesson helps prepared for him—Group Graded, Closely Graded, or Uniform. If the organization of your Sunday school permits, Closely Graded materials for Primaries, Juniors, and Intermediates should be provided. The weekly officers and teachers' meeting should train workers in effective use of the curriculum materials. Advance study of the teacher's helps and *The Sunday School Builder* will enable pastors and superintendents to call attention to especially helpful features.

V. OTHER OPPORTUNITIES FOR IMPROVEMENT OF TEACHING

A comprehensive church program of training provides many opportunities which will help teachers to become more effective.

1. *Make Full Use of the Church Study Course for Teaching and Training*

Teachers must constantly teach from the overflow if they are to be effective. By increasing the margin of information and inspiration they can become better teachers. The Church Study Course for Teaching and Training involves materials for enrichment as well as the development of skills. Opportunities should be provided for regular study of the general and department books on teaching. As new teachers are brought in, let it be the accepted policy to give them a working knowledge of teaching principles.

2. *Magnify the Bible Survey Plan*

It is generally agreed that one of the most acute needs in our Sunday school work is for a greater depth of Bible knowledge on the part of our teachers and officers. In order to give teachers, and others, a connected unified, overview of the textbook of the Sunday school, the Bible Survey Plan has been provided. It has met with great favor, and increasing numbers of churches are adopting the plan as an annual feature for the development of better teaching.

Within the framework of the Church Study Course for Teaching and Training, the Bible Survey Plan provides six units of study, based on six books found in categories 1 and 2. *The Book of Books* by H. I. Hester; *From Adam to Moses* by H. W. Tribble; *From Joshua to David* by John L. Hill; *From Solomon to Malachi* by Kyle M. Yates; *From Bethlehem to Olivet* by Hight C Moore: *From Pentecost to Patmos* by Hight C Moore. The plan involves the use of a kit of "Supplementary Study Helps for the Bible Survey Plan," which may be secured from a Baptist Book Store. These helps consist of work sheets to be used by students as the Bible itself is read. Reading through the entire Bible during the eight months' period; and filling in the workbook, which is primarily a study of the characters in the Bible and how they fit into the plan of God, will provide rich learning activities.

It is recommended that the pastor, or some other competent individual designated by him, teach the units in the Bible Survey Plan. A two-hour session for this special class, scheduled at some convenient time during each week for an eight-months' period, will provide necessary time for outside study and will permit a flexible schedule to avoid conflicts with other events in the church calendar. For further information about the plan, write to your state Sunday school secretary or to the Sunday School Department, Baptist Sunday School Board, Nashville, Tennessee.

3. *Promote Preview Studies*

A quarter-by-quarter advance study of the Sunday school lessons by all teachers is one of the most fruitful activities pastors and superintendents can provide. It will make the teaching more purposeful, unified, and productive. Appropriate guidance materials are available for every age group.

4. *Use January Bible Study Week*

Additional Bible study for all the church family is the ideal. Major on getting all Sunday school members from Junior age up into these special weeks of study. Textbook materials for Juniors and Intermediates are available. Guidance for units of teaching has been provided for use with Primary, Beginner, and Nursery children respectively.

5. *Encourage Proper Use of Visual Aids*

In the children's departments the planned use of flat pictures, objects, and activities is a valuable asset in teaching. Carefully selected slides, filmstrips, or motion pictures may be helpful, particularly in the departments which have assemblies. Good maps and chalkboards facilitate learning. The Sunday School Board through the Audio-Visual Aids Department is rapidly providing films and filmstrips for use in the teaching program. There are valuable audio-visual materials available for the training of teachers in the weekly officers and teachers' meetings and in study courses.

6. *Capitalize on Every Opportunity for Improvement*

Maintain a working church library and lead teachers, officers, and pupils in a well-planned reading program.

Hold personal conferences with teachers, scheduling regular times when they may seek personal guidance from the pastor, superintendent, or minister of education.

Urge attendance upon outside meetings, such as the Sunday school weeks at Ridgecrest or Glorieta, the state assembly, Sunday school conventions, and clinics. Workers should participate in the regular associational Sunday school meetings. Here opportunity is given for giving and receiving help and thus lifting the level of the work done.

Encourage every Sunday school officer and teacher to participate in the work of the Training Union and in the Woman's Missionary Union or the Brotherhood. Such activities will contribute to the personal enrichment of Sunday school workers and so result in improved teaching.

VI. The Teacher of Teachers

When we face the solemn obligations and the exciting opportunities of teaching we think of the Scripture passage, "Not by might, nor by power, but by my spirit, saith the Lord of hosts" (Zech. 4:6).

Jesus knew that teachers would need help, and so he sent the Holy Spirit to teach us. The Holy Spirit will guide us into truth we can only dimly perceive. He will strengthen our faltering efforts; he will open the way into the hearts of our pupils when doors seem closed.

With the unlimited sources of power at his command, a teacher should have assurance and courage. Let us use wisely the opportunities God has given us. Let us teach with conviction; let us teach by example; let us teach with joy.

WHAT WILL YOU DO?

This chapter offers very definite suggestions for improving the teaching in your Sunday school. Decide which of the suggestions need to be carried out more effectively in your church.

CHAPTER 8

8

A Church Going to the People

PEOPLE are not seeking churches. Perhaps the great multitudes of people never have sought the churches. They are disturbed and distraught, but they seem to avoid that which could provide the only remedy.

True, some are kept from church attendance through no choice of their own, but for whatever the reason, millions of people every Lord's Day are missing the spiritual blessing of Bible study and worship in the churches.

People are moving. Whole new centers of population are springing up away from the churches. It is estimated that during a twelve months' period 25 per cent of the population have moved into new dwellings. Some leave the home communities temporarily in pursuit of education, for business reasons, or in answer to the call into military service. What are churches to do for all these people?

Churches must seek people. We find nowhere in the New Testament that churches are to teach only those who seek us out! Churches must not wait. In the face of such conditions as we have considered and had pressed down upon us, we turn to the Sunday school for some effective ways to meet the highly complex conditions today. Surely the Sunday school has "come to the kingdom for such a time as this."

I. THROUGH VISITATION—BRING THE PEOPLE IN

A certain pastor received a unique present; it was a tie chain in the shape of a door knocker—symbolic of the ministry of a pastor and of an effective New Testament church. Certainly it is a symbol of a growing Sunday school. Without "knocking on doors," visiting in season and out of season, no school can hope to reach the unreached. The slogan of an advertising concern, "People go where they are invited, and stay where they are well treated," is suggestive for the ministry of our Sunday schools.

1. Visitation Embodies the Spirit of the New Testament

Christianity is an outgoing expression of an inner possession. The command of Christ, the example of our Saviour, and the practice of the early Christians agree that sharing with others in personal visitation is of central concern. Consider what the Bible has to say about visitation:

V The practice of Jesus (Matt. 9:35)
I The product of compassion (Matt. 9:36)
S The principle of the Great Commission (Matt. 28:19-20)
I The program of the early churches (Acts 13:1-3)
I The plan for enlisting people (Luke 14:23)
T The pattern for Christian service (John 20:21)
A The proof of religion (James 1:27)
T The path to pastoral success (Acts 5:42)
I The price of fruit bearing (John 15:16)
O The procedure in world missions (Mark 16:15)
O The preparation for evangelism (Luke 10:1-3)
N The partnership with Christ (Matt. 25:35-40) [1]

A study of these Scripture passages undergirds the conviction that visitation is in accordance with the spirit and command of the New Testament.

2. Visitation Will Improve the Work of a Sunday School

I consider visiting in our Sunday school program as I do cream and sugar in my diet—it improves almost anything!

Are we not very close to the heart of God and the heart of true religion when we practice visitation? "Pure religion and

[1] Based on material prepared by John T. Sisemore.

undefiled before God and the Father is this, To visit" (James 1:27). Visitation is the universally effective and available means of promulgating the faith. Visitation improves the work of a Sunday school by helping us hurdle certain barriers.

(1) *There is the barrier of limited numbers.*—We will teach more if we reach more. At the very best our churches now are teaching only a fraction of the people they ought to teach. Enlistment comes before enlightenment. Visitation puts our churches in contact with the people.

To be sure, we must be concerned about the quality of our teaching. We must never think of our work in terms of enrolment alone, neither can we afford to allow ourselves to think that there is incompatibility between reaching numbers of people and doing quality work. Our teaching program will never grow and expand to reach the world through a quality approach alone. Reaching and teaching must move together.

(2) *There is the barrier of limited understanding.*—Visitation brings increased information regarding the needs of pupils. Jesus "needed not that any should testify of man: for he knew what was in man" (John 2:25). His intimate knowledge of the heart condition and spiritual readiness of each individual guided him in his approach and in his immediate purpose. He did not teach everyone alike. Consider the way he dealt with Nicodemus. Think of his work with the woman at the well.

Our members all have similar basic needs and drives, but they are expressed in many ways. If we could know what is back of the conduct of various members, we would know better how to understand and deal with the individuals. Undesirable behavior is always a symptom of inner need.

(3) *There is the barrier of poor communication.*—Lack of access to the learner's heart is a serious problem. Unless the pupil lets you in, you're out!

The story of the Shunammite woman (2 Kings 4) is a clear illustration. When she found herself in a distressing experience she sought out Elisha, who had been a regular visitor in the home. The well-meant ministry of Gehazi, Elisha's servant, was rejected. But when she came to Elisha, the one with whom she had fellowship and whom she felt confident would be able to help her, she poured out her soul and opened her troubled heart.

Effective teaching requires a two-way street where the pupil comes to the teacher as well as the teacher goes to the pupil. Visitation develops a bond of fellowship and comradeship which alone makes real communication possible.

3. *Visitation Must Be Planned and Practiced*

Visitation pays big dividends. The Middle River Baptist Church in Maryland a few years ago had a membership of 84 and a Sunday school enrolment of 125. In eight years the Sunday school enrolment increased to 2,252, or an annual average increase of 281 for an eight-year period. An enlarged organization has contributed to growth, so has additional space. But after everything else had been added, it was regular, consistent, prayerful visitation that brought about such great results. It is reported that one man in the community said, "I believe I have been visited a hundred times by your church."

Consider some essentials in getting visiting done:

(1) *Elect a superintendent of enlargement.*—Anything as vital as visitation requires someone who will give time to supervise and promote it. Many Sunday schools have discovered the value of electing a superintendent of enlargement, with promoting visitation as his major responsibility. He should be one who himself knows how to visit and who visits! But he should also be one who knows how to enlist others.

(2) *Schedule a regular time in the calendar.*—When the

church adopts a regular visitation time, it helps to pinpoint the sense of responsibility for visiting. Select the best time for your church. Thursday seems to be an acceptable time, but whatever the day, make it definite in the calendar.

(3) *Make the program definite and practical.*—Here again, each church will need to work out its own plans. Some churches plan to visit at night only. Others arrange for visitation day to include morning, afternoon, and evening visitation times. Generally, men can be enlisted to do visitation best in the evenings. Perhaps a light supper could be arranged at the church so that those who visit in the evening could come directly from work and get an early start.

As a means of enlisting individuals definitely for participation in the program, some churches ask each Adult and Young People's class to sign up at least two members each Sunday to visit on the following Thursday. Of course, the department officers and teachers are expected to visit. The list of those who sign up on Sunday for definite visitation is turned in to the superintendent of enlargement. Last-minute reminders may be sent those who have agreed to visit.

(4) *Use reports and recognitions.*—Where there are specific plans for securing reports on visitation, many values follow. More visiting is done. Stimulation and encouragement are gained through shared experiences. Many churches provide some recognition for those who have performed faithfully their visitation responsibilities. Some churches use visitation honor rolls, others award certificates of honor to workers and pupils who participate in specified ways.

Nothing inspires quite so much as success. When the people know that visitation succeeds it is easier to get more visitation done; and visitation does succeed!

In a recent year, Tower Grove Baptist Church in St. Louis, Missouri, reported 33,465 visits, or an average of 644 personal visits each week. During that year there were 293 coming into the church by baptism, 286 by letter and 11 by statement, or a total of 590 additions to the church. The Sunday school attendance averaged 200 over the preceding year and the Sunday school enrolment had a net increase of 620. During one month when a special drive was given to visitation, 4,280 visits were made, and during that particular month 303 new members were added to the Sunday school enrolment.

II. THROUGH PROPER DEPARTMENTS—TAKE BIBLE STUDY TO THE PEOPLE

The preceding discussion has been concerned with going after people to bring them to the church house. But when this has been done, even to an exceptional degree, yet there is room for additional ministries to those who cannot attend the Sunday services.

1. *The Cradle Roll Department Is a Key to Unreached Parents*

A church that is interested in the babies and that sends capable and consecrated visitors regularly into the homes will be amply rewarded with response from parents.

The Cradle Roll department has appropriate teaching materials. The workers use *The Sunday School Builder* and *Living with Children*. The parents receive *Home Life* magazine and the appropriate series from *Messages to Cradle Roll Parents*.

The Cradle Roll department provides a ministry to parents for the benefit of the babies. The visitor is a teacher; the classroom is the home; the prize pupils are the mother and father.

To be a teacher of parents is of first rank importance. A personal message to every Cradle Roll worker would say, "Teachers of parents are the architects of tomorrow. That is the role you play, and could one ask a greater privilege?

Winning parents, guiding parents, encouraging parents is the special privilege reserved by your church for you."

The Cradle Roll department is a line of supply, discovering prospects for every department. Often it opens the way for reaching whole families. It offers superior evangelistic opportunities. It reaches many homes where parents are not Christians. It has ripe opportunity for spiritual ministry at times when hearts have been softened and made aware of need.

2. The Extension Department Offers Bible Study for Those Who Cannot Attend

Within easy reach there are literally millions of people who are constantly being passed by because it is impossible for them to attend the services of the church. Perhaps one out of five of the total possibilities for your Sunday school belong to the group of shut-ins (the elderly and ill) or shut-outs (Sunday workers).

The Extension department visitor is a teacher. The member studies the same lesson course he would use if he came to Sunday school. He receives the *Sunday School Extension Department Quarterly* and *Home Life* magazine. For blind members the Sunday School Board provides *The Braille Baptist* and *Intermediate Braille Baptist* free of charge, on specific request from the church. Since *The Braille Baptist* is printed in either braille grade 1½ or grade 2, the request must specify which grade the member can read. This information would be secured from the member.

The visitor, in his regular monthly visits, plans for Bible reading, prayer, and lesson study.

Pastors find able assistants in Extension department workers. Their ministry results in winning lost men and women to Christ, arousing the indifferent, promoting spiritual growth, and encouraging participation in the total program of the church through prayer and financial support.

3. *The Young People Away Department Holds on to Many*

Each year more than 400,000 Baptist Young People are temporarily away from home in college or in military service.

The purpose of the Young People Away department is to guarantee regular spiritual ministry and church contact for all Young People temporarily away from home. While it is counted as a department of the Sunday school, under the direction of the general superintendent, it is actually a joint enterprise of the Sunday school and Training Union. Both organizations should be represented in the officers of the Young People Away department. Members should receive both Sunday school and Training Union materials: *Open Windows, Home Life, Sunday School Young People* or *Sunday School Married Young People,* and *Baptist Young People.* Personal letters, news letters, birthday greetings, and other means of keeping in touch will make the YPA department an effective ministry.

Young people away from home are kept on the YPA roll until they return or establish permanent residence elsewhere. However, they will be counted in the Sunday school or Training Union enrolment of the home church only until word has been received that they have joined another Sunday day school or Training Union, as the case may be. The file cards should be designated as Ministry Card or Enrolment Card, in order to keep the record straight.

III. THROUGH NEW SUNDAY SCHOOLS—ESTABLISH CHURCHES WHERE THE PEOPLE ARE

By divine assignment, Christians through the churches are to occupy and tend the fields which are white unto harvest. The extent of the field is unmistakable. It includes the world. The priority is simultaneous. It may mean Hong Kong or Buenos Aires—or it may be just three blocks away!

If people are beyond the practical reach of a Baptist church there we have an obligation. We must take a Sunday school and church to them!

1. *People Are Scattered*

When Jesus looked on the multitudes he saw them scattered as sheep having no shepherd. Such is the condition of our rapidly increasing population. But scattered as they are, out into great new areas beyond the present reach of our churches, they are not out of the circle of God's love.

The need for vast numbers of Sunday schools, missions, and churches is evident. They are needed because the present number of churches is inadequate to the present population. They are needed because of the swelling population adding some two million people annually to the already large number of unreached and unchurched. They are needed in vast metropolitan areas like Los Angeles, where each week nearly 1,800 additional units of housing are occupied by families not there the week before. We need new churches because the territory of Southern Baptists is expanding. We now have churches or missions in all fifty states, and in pioneer areas the need for churches is staggering.

Contrary to what many believe to be true, increasing the number of churches does not reduce the size of existing churches, but it does mean more people reached and ministered to. In a typical association, largely rural with small towns and villages, the average membership for each Baptist church is larger than it was thirty years ago, even with twice the number of churches. Yet, the unchurched population of the association today equals the total population of thirty years ago.

2. *People Are Reached by New Churches*

As we have learned a long time ago in our Sunday school work, new units grow faster, win more people to Christ, provide more workers and develop members in stewardship. Exactly the same is true in new churches. A study was made to compare churches organized before 1950 with churches organized since 1950. The following chart summarizes what was found:

	Churches Organized Before 1950	Churches Organized Since 1950
Ratio of baptisms to membership	1 to 21.9	1 to 8.1
Sunday school enrolment as percentage of church membership	75.8	130.4
Training Union enrolment as percentage of church membership	24.2	52.4
Total gifts per member	$35.57	$58.66

Just to take one example from the chart, you will notice that the newer churches on the average have 130 people in Sunday school enrolment for every 100 church members. If all of the churches in the Southern Baptist Convention would do as well in this respect, our Sunday school enrolment in 1959 would have been well over 12,000,000 instead of 7,276,000. What would the enrolment of your Sunday school be on that same basis?

Measured by souls reached, workers enlisted, total gifts to the cause of Christ or any other means available, it is profitable for Southern Baptists to start new Sunday schools and churches by the thousands.

3. *Follow a "Bill of Rights" for New Churches*

When new Sunday schools, missons or new churches are established, it would be well to consider some basic rights that should be safeguarded.

(1) *A New Testament church, mission or chapel, has a right to be wellborn.*—It needs to be started by a mother church in a spirit of prayer and conviction that the Lord is directing the work.

(2) *A new work has a right to be properly located.*—We need to locate the people and find where new work is needed now. We also need to determine where people are going to be living in fast developing areas, and be there first with churches.

(3) *A new work has a right to be encouraged and protected.*—It should be under the sponsorship of a church, financially underwritten by that church, with provision of needed leadership to guarantee a worthy beginning.

4. *Starting a New Sunday School Opens the Way*

While a new work can quickly include a full educational and preaching program, the best way is to start with the Sunday school and build around that. Frequently the best way to start the new Sunday school is to start with a mission Vacation Bible school.

A church in a small village recently went out to a remote section of their community, held a Vacation Bible school and revival meeting, and started a branch Sunday school. Within the first month they were having an attendance of thirty people. There are multiplied hundreds of situations that could do the same.

The best way to start a Sunday school or a new work of any kind is through the church missions committee, on which the Sunday school superintendent should serve. The church committee should work in co-operation with the associational missions committee, on which the associational Sunday school superintendent should serve. With these two committees set up and functioning any church can find a proper way of starting a new work, with due consideration to all other churches involved.

Many associations have adopted as their goal establishing 10 per cent as many new Sunday schools each year as they have churches. Doubtless your church should start a new Sunday school, mission, or church this year.

5. *New Work Is Basic Missions*

Southern Baptists are committed to missions around the world. Where lost men are, there must we go. Through the life we ourselves have in Christ we are become new creatures who must share the Word of reconciliation with others.

Through the Foreign Mission Board, Southern Baptists are sending thousands of missionaries into other countries. The Home Mission Board with its vast army of missionaries provides for Southern Baptists an effective witness in the homeland for language groups, for undeveloped areas in city, association, for pioneer territory, and for many other areas of service.

But where is the mission enterprise centered? What feeds it, nourishes it, sustains it? What gives direction to it, develops it, expands it? The spirit of missions grows in our churches. From the time the Holy Spirit spoke to the church at Antioch, "Separate me Barnabas and Saul for the work whereunto I have called them," until the last missonary was appointed, the strategy of giving the gospel to the world has been through the churches.

Let the churches grow in concern for the lost world; let the missionary conscience of the churches become more sensitive; let the churches teach, preach, and practice missions; and God will have his Word proclaimed to the ends of the earth. We believe that "the light that shines the farthest burns brightest at home." Is it not equally true that "the light that burns the brightest at home shines the farthest"?

Southern Baptists are now engaged in one of the most exciting adventures in their history—an effort to extend the gospel to millions of people within our immediate reach through establishing 10,000 new churches and 20,000 missions by 1964. This effort could well be considered basic missions, for every new church and every new mission established increases the missonary zeal and compassion of the existing churches. It broadens the operational bases from which the gospel may be extended to all the millions of people now beyond our immediate reach.

Starting more Sunday schools, establishing missions, organizing new churches is basic missions, if by these means more lost people near and far learn the Word of God, hear the gospel preached and come to know Christ as Saviour and Lord. To do these things will not impede but accelerate missions at home and abroad.

Lostness is not a matter of geography. The teeming millions of lost people in the unchurched and underchurched areas of our land are just as lost as if they lived halfway around the globe. Compassionate concern for them, and practical steps taken to reach them, increases compassion for lost men everywhere. The record of new churches established in the past few years points up the fact that here will be found the most productive field for evangelism and the most zealous support for missions.

WHAT WILL YOU DO?

What will you do about the visitation program of your Sunday school?

What needs to be done about the work of the Cradle Roll, Extension, and YPA departments of your Sunday school?

How deep is your concern for people in the areas where your church should start new work? What are you willing to do?

CHAPTER 9

9

MORE Is the Word

THE QUESTION has been raised by some, perhaps with an element of the critical in it, "When will Southern Baptists get over their obsession with numbers?" The answer is, "Never, we would devoutly pray!" Never—so long as we are in the midst of the unreached! Never—so long as we seek people to glorify God! Never—so long as we reach people for Bible study, for the preaching of the Word, for Christian training, for Christ and his service! Never—so long as we recall the words in the parable Jesus told: "Go out into the highways and hedges, and compel them to come in, that my house may be filled" (Luke 14:23).

Churches everywhere can do more for the glory of God—can reach, teach, win, and develop more people for their good and the blessing of the world.

Yes, we need more! More of everything that is good! More teachers, more preachers, more classes, more departments, more churches, more Sunday schools, more visitation, more Bible teaching, more Bible studying, more praying, more planning, more organization, more soul-winning, more dedication, more training, more all-out effort to do the will and work of Christ than ever before!

The answer to the needs, problems, and opportunities of our churches is in a word—M-O-R-E!

MANPOWER, **O**RGANIZATION, **R**EADINESS, **E**NTHUSIASM.[1]

[1] Acknowledgement is given Dr. Julian T. Pipkin, state Sunday school secretary of Georgia, for arrangement of acrostic.

137

I. MANPOWER

Good Sunday schools do not happen. They are built by consecrated, trained workmen. Any church, we believe, has within it enough human resources to accomplish God's purpose through that church. Certainly the divine resources are there, the compelling commission is there, the field of service is there.

There seems to be a certain divine order in the Christian program. Enlargement precedes teaching; teaching comes before evangelism; evangelism comes before enlistment; enlistment comes before fruitful Christian living and service. This is the strategy of the Sunday school.

There is a divine pattern for finding workers. Jesus told us what it was—"Pray ye." Surely today our first great need is to follow Christ's directive and pray for the workers we need. To look prayerfully for workers is to find them.

It was during an enlargement campaign. The pastor studied the impressive census returns. There was an immediate need for twice the workers he now had, but he had gone over his church roll time and again. Some could do the work, but would they respond? Did he have faith enough?

On Wednesday evening when the needs had been presented this pastor called on his members to join him in praying for workers to do the work God had given to be done. They prayed for faith to find the workers and for God's spirit to touch the hearts of those who should answer the call to service. It was like a revival. The workers were found and when during the week the pastor and superintendent called upon them to accept places of responsibility many answered, "I've been seeking for an opportunity like this—it is an answer to prayer!"

The people Christ needs for his work have a deep need for service opportunities. In visiting a church, I was greeted by an old friend whom I had not seen for several years. In the course of the conversation, it developed that for a number of reasons she had dropped various places of responsibility in the church and was inactive for a time. It was a dreary experience. She felt a deep sense of dissatisfaction with herself. Two years before, she had recommitted herself to the task and was back at work teaching again. She brightened as she said it: "I like myself better now!"

II. ORGANIZATION

William P. Phillips used to tell of the advertisement used by a certain taxicab company. After enumerating their various services, they concluded with the statement, "We are an organized responsibility!" Is your Sunday school adequately organized for its responsibility? Have you planned big enough for the present opportunities? for the days ahead?

The host of unreached people has grown in our nation to more than 130 million who are enrolled in no Sunday school. The Sunday school enrolment of all denominations is not keeping up with the population growth. We must grow, and grow faster this year.

Is your church ready to reach the multitudes in your community for Bible study and for Christ? They must be provided for before they can be reached.

Have you considered the power of the Cradle Roll department to reach homes for Christ? Half of our churches, as yet, do not have such a department functioning.

Do you have a place and program for Nursery children that will meet their needs and pull their parents to church? Every church should have at least four Nursery departments: one for the infants, one for the toddlers, one for the two-year-olds, one for the three-year-olds.

Has your church discovered that Beginner children can be reached in as great numbers per year as perhaps any other age group? The great increase in population that is still centered in the younger age groups makes provision for

Beginners an immediate imperative in all of our churches.

Do you make sure each year that your provision for Primary children is adequate to hold every Beginner child who is promoted?

Juniors will attend! Do you have enough classes and departments for Juniors to allow for growth? Start enough Junior classes to permit an enrolment of only about five for each class. Add four or five prospects and watch your Junior enrolment grow.

Have you proved that Intermediates can be reached and held for Bible study if only a church will maintain as many classes and departments for them as for Juniors?

Have you considered your Young People and provided for them in keeping with their needs? There are classifications of Young People that require special provision if they are to be reached—the seventeen-year-olds, the older single Young People, the married Young People, the Young People in college centers, and those who are away in military service.

Has your church really "gone into Adult business" seriously and made possible reaching the host of Adults for Bible study? If the other members of the family are to be reached, Adults are the key. In most churches there should be four times the number of working units to reach the Adult possibilities we have now.

Have you claimed the practical use of the Extension department to reach that 18 per cent of the population who cannot attend the Sunday sessions of your church?

Has your church gone beyond its present building and location to provide branch stations, chapels, and missions in an effort to provide Bible study for the multitudes who are beyond the practical reach of the present churches? Tomorrow may be too late for many of them.

Today's lost millions wait for the impact of a united Bible study program. They will be reached, taught, and won when our churches everywhere provide adequate space, programs, and workers in keeping with the opportunities God has given.

III. READINESS

A motto of Paul's life was, "I am ready" (Rom. 1:15). Readiness to serve must characterize the enlisted manpower of our churches. This readiness involves many things: personal willingness, a Christian faith and experience to share, an appreciation of the values of human personality, and a growing knowledge of effective ways to communicate ideas.

God never uses anyone against his will any more than he saves anyone against his will. A Christian who expects God to bless his efforts must be perfectly willing to accept the demands of his office as well as the honor.

What are the demands? Perhaps to state it in a sentence we would say to be a sincere Christian and loyal church member without reservation. One who grudgingly accepts an office, who assumes a place of service with reservations, could hardly be counted a worthy representative of Christ and his church. Jesus had something to say about one who had put his hand to the plow and looked back. Hesitant service lacks power as it lacks heart.

1. Sunday School Officers and Teachers Are Christ's Workmanship

"For we are his workmanship, created in Christ Jesus unto good works" (Eph. 2:10). We are his handiwork, the trophy of his redeeming love. Christ has saved us to serve. The purpose in our salvation is to share in the purpose of Christ for the salvation of every soul.

2. Sunday School Officers and Teachers Are Christ's Workmen

We are not ordinary workmen working at an ordinary task. We are superior workmen working at a supreme task.

All of us should strive to be the kind of "approved" worker Paul speaks of (2 Tim. 2:15). We are not working for ourselves at our own appointed tasks; we are working for Christ under appointment of the King! We are appointed to handle his word aright. We are to qualify for his approval.

3. Sunday School Officers and Teachers Are Obligated to Grow

Improvement is our watchword. Our personal obligation to Christ indicates it; our position as God's workmen requires it; our purpose to guide growing life demands it. "Grow in grace, and in the knowledge of our Lord and Saviour Jesus Christ" (2 Peter 3:18).

Thus we begin to see our calling, begin to glimpse the glories and requirements of it, the privileges and the constraints. The call to Christian service is the call for improvement, and the beginning point for better work is better workmen. Will you be that workman in your church?

IV. ENTHUSIASM

Workers in God's vineyard need heart power, first and foremost. The word "enthusiasm" has a significant meaning. It comes from Greek words meaning, "God in us." For one to be truly enthusiastic, then, is to have within him God's power and God's spirit in his work.

1. We Need to Be Excited About Teaching the Word

There is nothing wrong with our Sunday schools that genuine, Spirit-born excitement cannot cure. The reason for failure is not so much lack of ability as it is lack of passion. The "one thing I do" in Paul's personality was a strong factor in his service as an apostle of Christ.

What gets the creative process started is excitement—a passion, a yearning, a consuming ambition, and internal compulsion of some kind that stirs a man up.[1]

Do we not have something worth getting excited about? What could be more exciting than the privilege of teaching the Word of God—of "holding forth the word of life"?

Frank C. Baxter, professor of English at the University of Southern California, says of those teachers who contributed the most to his life:

They were obsessed and excited people, and the things they talked about were not sterile dead bones of factual learning . . . Their lips, touched with fire, spoke about the subjects that were electrically alive for them. I and my fellows were permitted to overhear and in the magic catalyst of the classroom caught fire from the sparks they struck off.[2]

If teachers of history, literature, mathematics, and science can become so excited and enthusiastic about their subjects (and they do); and if their effectiveness as teachers is determined in a large measure by their enthusiasm for their subjects (and it is); then surely, under God, we can become far more excited about the wonderful Book God has given us to teach.

2. We Need to Be Excited About Winning the Lost

Henry Bilbrey became a Christian in October, 1959, at thirty-seven years of age. After Christ came into his life, his whole personality changed. Prior to this he had lived more or less as an introvert, indifferent to people. After becoming a Christian, he led seventeen of his neighbors and friends to Christ, in addition to being responsible for four others who joined the church by letter.

He was a shift worker at the Victor Chemical Company and used every available moment—beginning sometimes as

[1] Elmer G. Leterman, *The Art of Selling* (New York: Harper and Bros., 1957).

[2] Houston Peterson, *Great Teachers* (New Brunswick, N. J.: Rutgers University Press, 1947).

early as six in the morning until late at night—to witness to others of the saving power of Christ in his life.

The life of Henry Bilbrey as a Christian was pressed into just five and one-half months of service, but it is a glorious example of what a soul-winner with a passion for the lost can do. At his funeral service two men he had been seeking to win made public their profession of Christ. The following Sunday two others came. Henry Bilbrey literally won his whole street to the Lord!

After his death the work goes on. Within a month a total of more than thirty people have come into the church as a result of his influence. Two notebooks were found containing the names of thirty-six prospects with whom he had already visited and prayed. The neighbors and friends who have come to Christ through his efforts have agreed that they would like to carry on this work with the thirty-six prospects he left behind, and they are adding more of their own.

Henry Bilbrey was a member of Calvary Baptist Church in Nashville, Tennessee. The church, through the Sunday school officers and teachers, has been successful in evangelism. A recent study of the decisions made at Calvary indicates that fifty-two of the sixty-four persons joining on profession of faith, and thirty-one of the thirty-six coming by letter were members of the Sunday school.

3. *How Can We Become More Evangelistic?*

The answer to this question is of deep significance for the continued fruitful ministry of your church.

Adopt the goal: "Every worker a personal soul-winner."

Let the regular visitation program include specific emphasis on unaffiliated and unsaved prospects.

Work for prayer lists prepared and used by every Christian member of every class.

Promote widespread participation in all extra Bible study

opportunities offered by the church, such as January Bible Study Week, special Bible studies offered by class groups, the Bible Survey Plan, Operation Home Study, and others.

Urge particular support of all church revival meetings.

It is increasingly apparent that evangelists are discovering that both preparation for a revival meeting and the actual support of a revival meeting can be best accomplished and undergirded through the use of the Sunday school forces. This practice uses an evangelistic organization already set up, assures greater evangelistic results, and enriches the ministry of Sunday school workers.

The major opportunities of the Sunday school in soul-winning bring inescapable accountability. We have an opportunity; let us make the most of it.

The world has yet to see what our churches can do in winning multitudes of lost people by developing the Sunday school workers into a major evangelistic force.

WHAT WILL YOU DO?

That is the question: What will you DO? What difference will the study of this book make in the outreach of your Sunday school?

END WITH PRAYER

THAT WE WILL BE

PERSONAL

SOUL WINNERS!

Teaching Suggestions

THIS BOOK has been written as guidance material for use in connection with the efforts of any church to increase its outreach. It will be effective to make the class periods a workshop, or continued project, in which the class members seek to formulate plans in answer to the over-all problem: *What should our church do, through its Sunday school, to increase its outreach to the unreached?* This book would be resource material to guide in determining the answers to the problem.

It will be well to have the census completed and tabulated before the study of this book begins. On the first night display the chart from chapter 3. Columns 1, 2, 3, 4, 7, and 10 should be filled in from the Sunday school enrolment records and the census tabulation.

Chapters 1 and 2

In a project, teacher and class members must mutually agree on a worthwhile purpose and become personally involved in the activities needed to carry it to completion. If chapters 1 and 2 are studied with the figures in columns 1, 2, 3 of the chart before the class, the challenge should be very real. Teacher and class should come to the end of the first two periods with a deep conviction that, together, they must discover and carry out the answer to the questions: How many people is our Sunday school responsible for as of now? How can we provide for and reach all these people (column 2) who are our responsibilities, but who are not now enrolled in our Sunday school?

MOTION PICTURES: *Reaching Out; Lift Up Your Eyes; Endued with Power*

FILMSTRIP: *The Church Council*

Chapter 3

It will be well to make clear how the figures in column 2 of the chart have been secured. If the census returns were not available for the first class session, try to secure full information by the second evening and bring column 3 up to date.

Study the principles by which a Sunday school grows. Discuss those which need particular attention in the church, or churches, represented in the class.

Lead class members to face the question squarely: Will we make room in our hearts, in our plans, in our space, in the outreach of our program? Seek to lead workers to determine what

146

should be done in each area named, and to come individually, to full commitment to do the things that ought to be done.

FILMSTRIP: *Laws of Sunday School Growth*

Chapter 4

Lead the class members to apply the suggested organization for each group, as given in this chapter to the figures in column 3 of the chart. Together work out the figures for columns 6, 8, 11, and 12. The results may seem staggering, and the class may wish to pause for prayer. Use the content of the chapter to lead the members to a holy determination to discover needed workers. Challenge them to pray for vision, faith, and wisdom for themselves. Challenge them also to united, unrelenting, specific prayer for the needed workers.

FILMSTRIP: *How to Enlist Sunday School Workers*

Chapter 5

A study of columns 5 and 8 of the chart from chapter 3 will point up a very real problem: How can we find space? Use the chart of space needs in chapter 5 to determine, first what space your church needs for each age group to make full provision for its present responsibilities (enrolled plus prospects, column 3). Use the table under "Population Trends" (chap. 5) to dream about the number of responsibilities the church will have in each age group within the next ten years.

Raise the question: What steps should we take now to get available space? Based on the guidance given in chapter 5, lead the class to make plans worthy of what God expects.

Divide the class into groups to explore the building, or buildings available. See which group can locate the most and best usable space.

MOTION PICTURE: *Take Time to Plan*

Chapter 6

Help the class to see why goals are important. Then "nail down" the points discussed so far by filling in the goal sheet together. Use copies of the sheet given in this chapter or the one in the planning booklet for Preparation Week.

To arrive at goals for the whole Sunday school, meet by departments or by age groups to determine the age-group goals. Meet together and combine these goals, making adjustments if necessary, to determine the total Sunday school goals.

Chapter 7

Raise the question: How can we be ready to do our best teaching for all the people we are trying to reach? Discuss chapter 7 to find some answers. Lead the class to list the things they resolve to do or to ask their church to do. They may plan to—

(1) Determine what diplomas and seals each worker has.

(2) Make up "Workers in Training" charts.

(3) Request the church nominating committee to locate a Sunday school superintendent of training.

(4) Plan the major training activities for the year.

(5) Set training goals for the school and by departments.

FILMSTRIP: *The Weekly Officers and Teachers' Meeting; The Christian Teacher; Church Officers at Work; How to Train Sunday School Workers*

Chapter 8

Seek to lead the class to agree on a systematic plan for visitation which they will recommend to the church for adoption and pledge to support.

Lead the class to consider the work of the Cradle Roll, Extension, and Young People Away departments in their church. Discuss ways in which the work in these departments should be strengthened, and decide how these improvements may be implemented.

Use the discussion about new Sunday schools to lay on the hearts of the class that *their* church needs to be working now to start at least one more new Sunday school. If the church missions committee has some specific place to recommend, arrange for a report to that effect.

If there has been no previous planning, perhaps the most effective response you can secure will be the agreement to pursue the matter in prayer and to urge the church to appoint a "live-wire" missions committee.

FILMSTRIP: *The Sunday School and the 30,000 Movement*

MOTION PICTURE: *How to Visit*

Chapter 9

The presentation of this chapter should lead to deepened resolve, more earnest prayer, and renewed dedication to do the things which, during this study, the class has agreed need to be done.

For Review and Examination

Chapter 1

1. Mention three ways churches may fulfil their mission to the multitudes.
2. In what ways does the multiplying population affect our churches?
3. Discuss a church's contact with the multitudes.
4. What would you say should be the relationship between growth in numbers and improvement in quality of work being done by our churches?

Chapter 2

5. Comment on the functions of the church prescribed by Jesus.
6. How would you describe the distinctive purposes of the Sunday school?
7. State briefly how Southern Baptists' conception of the use of the Sunday school helps build strong churches.
8. What are some ways by which a Sunday School may be tested?

Chapter 3

9. Mention some values of finding a prospect for the Sunday school.
10. Give at least six constant sources of growth for the Sunday school.
11. What are the most important steps in preparing for a good census?
12. In keeping with suggestions made in chapter 3, how can you make room for growth in your Sunday school?

Chapter 4

13. Show the importance of securing more Sunday school workers; indicate the need for more church members to be enlisted to work.
14. Mention some requirements for effective leadership.
15. What are some practical steps a church should take in discovering and enlisting enough workers?
16. Outline a good program of training which should be provided for Sunday school workers.

Chapter 5

17. What is meant by "Build for the Baptist Program"?
18. What are some needed attitudes about space?
19. How may a church get the maximum use of available space?
20. What factors need to be taken into account in providing an adequate building for the Sunday school program?

Chapter 6

21. Discuss the purposes of Preparation Week; how may Preparation Week be made more effective in your church?
22. What types of goals should be set for your Sunday school work each year?
23. Describe how the Standards must be used wisely.
24. Show how Sunday school records may help get better work done.

Chapter 7

25. List the seven major objectives of Christian teaching and training.
26. How are these objectives to be used effectively in the Sunday school?
27. Mention some significant values of a weekly officers and teachers' meeting.
28. Briefly describe the Bible Survey Plan.

Chapter 8

29. Show how visitation will improve the work of the Sunday school.
30. What is the distinctive purpose of (1) the Cradle Roll department? (2) the Extension department? (3) the YPA department?
31. Why is it so important to establish new Sunday schools and churches?

Chapter 9

32. Why do you feel Southern Baptists must reach more people?
33. How can your Sunday school become more effective in evangelism?